Mule Kicks

*An Outdoorsman's Moments
of Grace, Love, and
New Perspectives*

John Odell

PUBLISHED BY PSALM 23:2, LLC

All inquiries should be addressed to
castingnetsfellowship@gmail.com

Paperback ISBN: 979-8-9932820-1-5
ebook ISBN: 979-8-9932820-2-2
Hardcover ISBN: 979-8-9932820-0-8

Edited by Kate Petrella
Cover and book design by Barbara Aronica
Cover art by Mary Tucker Southerland

This book is dedicated to everyone who helped build my love for the outdoors. Many names and faces appear throughout these pages of stories and memories. Mostly, I want to dedicate this to Garrett Harris, my great fishing buddy, who overcame a lot of battles to become an outstanding man, hard worker, wonderful father, and passionate fisherman. I'll never catch another smallmouth without seeing you grinning in the background, brother.

CONTENTS

FOREWORD

If, like me, you love to hunt and fish, or if you grew up in the out-doors spending time with friends and family, you are always inter-ested in hearing others' stories. You want to listen to their tales, learn of their unique encounters, and understand their interpreta-tion of these experiences that we all enjoy. It helps you gauge your own recollections. But it's not that we want to outdo each other. No sir. We inherently want to ensure that others are getting as much out of their special times as we do. And we want to know if per-haps others view glorious nature and the outdoors like we do. And maybe, just maybe, we may pick up a few pointers or get ideas as to how to better partake in our own blessed times outside.

With this curiosity, I began to read *Mule Kicks: An Outdoors-man's Moments of Grace, Love, and New Perspectives.* I've always liked mules. They are genuine, hard-working, solid, and reliable. If you invest time in a mule, he will do you right. The same holds for this book. And when you need to understand your real place and what is important, a mule may let you know—with a kick—what is important. And that is what John Odell does in this book. He lets you know, through his eyes, that what he has indeed learned is important, through all of his times outdoors.

Through various remembrances, John takes you to places all over, from the northeast coast to Mexico, to duck havens in Tennessee, and to revered haunts in eastern North Carolina. But it's not the places that you come away thinking about. It's the times with friends and family. It's precious moments spent with a son and his friend in a duck blind. It's the bond between a dog and his owner and the recognition we all have of that relationship. Maybe it's being caught off guard by the hammering of several gobblers within a few yards as dawn approaches. Or maybe it's understanding as a young father that the time spent with your family in a remote cabin is priceless.

From remembering some entertaining turkey conservation practices when he was a boy to fishing our coastal rivers for trout and drum with his family, John reminds us of what matters. As a father, he relays to us how the outdoors has benefited not only him, but also his children. His stories of experiences with them and time spent with his own father bring forth our own memories. John helps us once again remember that intricate, beautiful, and oftentimes mysterious nature can be the healer for everything. It soothes us with comfort, laughter, and reflection, as John points out in his stories.

In *Mule Kicks*, we are taken along to different places in eastern NC and beyond. But the real travel is not over land; it is in our minds. As John describes times spent outdoors with his friends and family, we think of our own. And we are once again reminded that we have been given God's gift, the great outdoors, for a reason.

If you feel closer to family, to God, and to yourself when you are out there hunting or fishing, you will enjoy John's stories. I certainly did.

Bill Fentress

Author of *The Yellow Honeysuckle Is the Sweetest* and *It's Not the Dirt*

PREFACE

As a boy, growing up in rural Surry County, North Carolina, I spent every waking moment of my life outdoors. I was either catching frogs and snakes in the woods, catching crawdads in the creek, or spending time in the garden with my Pa, trying to learn the secrets of growing the perfect tomato plant. My brother, who was my built-in babysitter, always made sure I was outside doing something. My dad was a fisherman, so my preteen and teenage years were spent in a trout stream or a farm pond, catching whatever would bite. These moments molded me into the man I would ultimately grow up to be.

I attended NC State University, where I met many people who became lifelong friends—and where I met the woman who would become my wife. After college, I moved to Greenville, NC, where I spent fifteen years working as a flock advisor for Perdue Farms. This job allowed me to explore all of the beautiful places eastern NC had to offer. In 2019, when my son was diagnosed with Type 1 diabetes, my wife and I decided that one of us had to make a career change to allow us to be closer to home during the day, in case he needed help while he was at school. It came as a blessing that my cousin, who knew about our situation, offered me a job selling commercial and agricultural insurance for his agency. This allowed me the opportunity to continue to provide for my family, while also being able to be at home to support my son. Today, my son is a teenager and my daughter is in second grade. We have an amazing life and a supportive extended family. I am aware of how lucky I am to have gone through all of the obstacles presented to me and still be in a position to be happy, healthy, and able to do what I love: spend as much time as possible outdoors. My wife grew up in a family of hunters, so she naturally understands my passion.

As a man with plenty of time in the woods under my belt, I have only recently begun the practice of soaking in the moments and trying not to let special times pass by unnoticed. Luckily, as someone who has journaled my endeavors in the outdoors for nearly twenty years, I have a lot of opportunity to reflect while I am writing. Even in times when I am rushing to put words on a page, almost like doing a chore, it is still a time of reflection. The older I get, the less I care about the "success" of a hunt through the scope of animals harvested. I now consider the success to come in the form of a memory made and a bond solidified with someone special to me, whether it be family or friend.

The little things involved in hunting and fishing brand a memory in my brain. The thrill of tricking a fish into biting your lure, and the excitement of never really knowing exactly what species it may be, or even how big it may be, are all exciting. Hearing a turkey respond to a call with a quick gobble, cutting you off mid-cluck, is a moment in nature when you feel truly connected to a wild animal. Tracking a buck through the woods, following the blood trail, then knowing you are getting close as you smell the odor emitted by the tarsal glands during the rut. You can't experience these from watching a hunting show. Some hunters take these moments for granted, but I never do.

I am, by nature, what most would consider a waterfowler. I participate in the other activities of an outdoorsman to pass the time, but no matter if it is mid-December or the Fourth of July, I am always pondering a duck. The work in the swamps to clear holes in the summer, planting food options and planning where to place blinds in an impoundment, installing wood duck boxes in the spring, and even shooting skeet in the off season to keep my skills in order—these things keep my motor running, and that isn't even during the hunting season.

There is a period between turkey season in early May and dove season in early September that we North Carolina waterfowl hunters all refer to with disdain as the "100 Day War." This is the only time of the year when you can't actively chase a wingshooting opportunity with a shotgun in our state. I am always chomping at the bit when dove season arrives, just to knock the dust off the gun and to officially welcome back the season of bird hunting.

Once duck season is here and in full swing, there is nothing like it in the hunting world. You can be social in the blind, hanging out with friends while doing something you love. You get caught up in watching a working bird react to a call, trying to understand his body language as you try to communicate, doing everything you can to persuade him to come closer. The colors of a late season, full-plumage duck is something that nothing else can compare to. A bull pintail in his full January tuxedo is such a fine specimen, I often catch myself handling him with extra care, as if I am trying to preserve him in his state as long as possible.

The deep thought that goes into the planning of where to hunt and where to place the decoys is one of my favorite aspects. You can scout, look at weather forecasts, and discuss til the sun comes up, and sometimes you are still wrong. There have been days where I scouted and saw nothing, but the next day ducks were every-where. In that same breath, though, I have to add that I've seen it the other way around as well. Decoy placement, regardless of what your buddy who is in a hurry says, is an art. If you fly a drone over ducks, or pay attention to them socializing on the water from a distance, you can see that their activity is not random. There is a method to the madness that must be unlocked to get the full potential of a hunt.

The thrill of the shot is special, because shooting an animal that is actively flying away from you is not easy. Once you've done the preseason work to get the spot ready, have built and brushed the blind and planted the food, and then when the time comes have set the decoys, you still have to finish the job by making the shot.

When it is all said and done, countless hours and dollars have been poured into every duck that you hold after a successful hunt, and what an amazing way to spend your money, and your time. As outdoorsmen, we are conservationists at heart, so we donate to the organizations we choose and invest time to ensure that not only our own hunting spots, but everyone else's too, are successful. This community is unrivaled among others. Yes, there may be some competition from time to time, and there are always a few bad apples, but all in all, it is truly a community. If you are ever at some social event with your wife in the summer, and maybe you went knowing none of the other folks that were going to be there, try this trick. Look at the other guys there closely. There will be some obvious signs, like maybe a camo hat or a truck in the parking lot with a Ducks Unlimited sticker, but there are also more subtle hints. If you see a guy who looks like he'd rather be anywhere else, sipping a bourbon while standing beside a significant other who looks far too attractive to be with him, go talk to him. If he has dog hair all over his vest, go talk to him. These are clues that he is in fact a duck hunter himself. Trust me, your time spent at the party will then be far more enjoyable.

INTRODUCTION

After nearly twenty years of writing a journal entry for every time I went hunting or fishing, the hustle and bustle of life began to make writing those entries seem like a chore. I would often forget for a few weeks, try to back date, and then write multiple entries in one sitting. Details began to not be as clear, and to be honest, the labor of actual handwriting began to feel too cumbersome.

I made the decision to start typing my entries on my laptop. Although this didn't feel as genuine, the process was much easier and I felt more comfortable going into detail, as typing is far easier and more enjoyable than writing by hand.

On my first entry, I started typing and the words were flowing with more description and detail than ever before. My wife was getting ready for bed, and as she walked through the room, I mentioned to her how much I was enjoying this new process. Somewhat in jest, she casually said, "You should just keep writing. Maybe you could write a book." Over the years, she had read some of my journal entries, and she always enjoyed my perspective in these writings. I thought maybe she was joking, but before she left the room, she doubled down.

"I'm serious, I think you could write a great book. I bet people would love to read some of your stories," she said, as she walked into the bedroom. As I sat there, pondering her words, I thought, "Why not?!" On that night, I started typing, and before I knew it, midnight had far passed and I had more than twenty pages written about so many scattered thoughts it seemed like a lost cause. Finally, after what seemed like hours, I went to bed. I was both excited and overwhelmed at the idea of possibly trying this.

For the next several months, I spent all of my free time, mostly after the rest of the house was asleep, trying to get my message on paper while also trying to decipher exactly what I wanted to say. After I had enough structure and information in place, I knew it was time for the next step.

I knew of an author who shared some mutual friends, so I decided I should just reach out to see if he were willing to share any knowledge. To my surprise, Bill Fentress was not only willing to help me with the process, but he ended up being my biggest supporter. His words pushed me to really focus and finish this project, while also helping me figure out the process of completing the book.

Through what can only be described as more Divine Intervention, I was introduced to the perfect editor, one who was very experienced in editing works about outdoor life. Suddenly, this was something I was no longer doing as a project to pass time. This became my passion, and I felt the urge to do everything I could to get my words on paper for others to see.

I have thoroughly enjoyed this process, and I hope every reader can get something positive out of these pages.

Mule Kicks

CHAPTER 1

The First Mule Kick

At first glance, it's just another morning in the duck blind on another Saturday in January. These days become so common and familiar during long, grinding duck seasons that it is easy for them to be taken for granted.

Today, though, is different. As we broke ice on the way across the cypress cutover, finding our way to the blind in the dark and cold, I had a different feeling than I normally do. I've experienced so many things while hunting, it seems hard for anything to stand out these days. I've seen some of North America's most beautiful offerings, have seen many a kid's first duck, and unfortunately even witnessed someone's last.

Treating a duck hunt like another day clocking into work is easy, but sometimes a hunt kicks you in the chest like an angry mule and corrects your perspective back to where it needs to be. This morning just so happened to be the morning of my son's thirteenth birthday. He has hunted with me on this property in Northampton County his whole life. We swaddled him up in blankets in the corner of the blind when he was three, as my only option to hunt while my wife was in anesthesia school was if he went along with me.

Luckily for me, he loved it as much as I did. He shot his first duck here when he was five, water swatting a wood duck on the pond at the cabin. His first deer was shot in the back food plot when he was seven, where he dropped a spike in his tracks with a .243.

A year later, his first turkey came in the spring in the same food plot. Our family was practicing "social distancing" during the spring of 2020, as COVID-19 was the topic of all discussions. What better place to hide out than in the little generator-powered cabin, where we could fish and hunt and spend time playing board games with the family. We snuck out one evening and had a gang of jakes bombard the decoy. After we enjoyed the show, my son rolled one and we celebrated as if we'd won the World Series that night.

Now, this morning of his first day as a teenager, was another first. This year, he had asked to invite a friend on his birthday hunt. Historically, these hunts had just been family occurrences. My father-in-law owns the property, and my brothers-in-law and I spend a lot of time here year-round, both working and hunting.

As a boy approaches being a teenager, the influence of friends begins to mold him nearly as much as family does. I was proud to see that my son had a buddy who shared the same passion for the outdoors, so I was excited to see them hunt together. Once we got to the hole where the blind was, the friend's dad and I set the boys up in the blind and busted out a hole in the ice to set a few motion decoys to keep the hole open.

I sat in my seat, sweating a little from the walk, while also freezing in the wind, and we all sat back to await the arrival of legal shooting time. I expected to see a few ducks, as I had scouted the previous day and knew we were holding a few birds. Our typical mallards hadn't showed up yet, so the wood ducks were going to have to fill our bucket this morning, or so I thought.

At exactly five minutes before shooting time, a drake black duck announced his presence with a low quack, then descended from the heavens right into our hole and started chuckling. The boys immediately perked up, as did I. Then, the mallards started a pre-light show that you only see in this swamp about every two or three years. It wasn't like we had hundreds flying around, but there were plenty, and they were all working our spread like their lives depended on it, as it was the only open water in the entire swamp. From every direction, we had pairs, singles and even a few large groups flying lower than the tree tops, looking in desperation for their landing spot. The sound of cutting wings kept everyone's attention locked in on the upcoming task of the hunt.

As any duck hunter knows, the minutes leading up to legal shooting time can last as long as entire vacation days. My son kept asking me to check the time, but it was creeping. Finally, I just told him to watch and enjoy—this sight is what duck hunters see when they close their eyes to sleep at night.

The next two minutes were silent in the blind. We had hens highballing as they flew through the spread, big groups cupping up and landing within what seemed like arm's reach, and duck chatter from every direction. I heard the boys laugh and gasp as they kept looking at each other, so excited about the moment, without even firing a shot yet.

That's when the mule showed up, kicking me right in the chest like he sometimes does. *This* is what I'll remember when I'm reminiscing about duck hunts in forty years, and this is the type of stuff my son will tell his kids one day, I hope while sitting in this same swamp.

You can't completely experience life as a hunter without repeatedly putting yourself out there. Some days you wonder why you got out of bed, and some days you can't imagine there being any place you'd rather be. As I always remind my son on mornings when he wants to sleep in, you never regret going, but you'll always regret missing out. You've got to get up and go, in case you witness something like this that will live in your head forever.

That hunt was one of our best ever at this swamp. Wood ducks decoyed all morning, and the boys made some great shots. Mallards and black ducks put on a display, and far too many of them got too close for their own good. We shot plenty of wood ducks, several mallards, a beautiful drake black duck, and even had several flocks of geese finish in our laps. The final volley of the morning included five Canadas flying over, as they often do here. We always see these guys, but rarely can we get them to come in. This morning, though, we had the advantage of open water. They made one pass, then turned on a dime. My son actually held me off on the shot, as I was ready as soon as they were in range. He made the right call though, because in ten seconds, they were at 10 yards. We jumped up, and in a split second, we had five on the water. We capped the morning off with bacon-fried honey buns and some photos. Then we all went our separate ways with a moment that will live in our memories for a lifetime.

CHAPTER 2

Setting the Scene

As a man over forty, I have experienced a lifetime of friendships. Some have lasted since middle school, while others have just started in the past year. When I was a young man, much like my son is now, friendships were built around sports and school activities. I often found myself befriending someone I had nearly zero in common with just because of the convenience of doing so.

I grew up with a phenomenal father as a role model. He was a family-first man, but he could also make friends with a stranger in a second. He had friends from the fanciest country clubs all the way to the guys that couldn't seem to stay out of their own way and lived in trouble. They all loved my dad for his honesty and true ability not to judge.

I adopted this outlook as a young man and made friends from every grade and every walk of life. My childhood has such random memories of times with friends that I sometimes can't piece together what was real and what was imagined.

My friend group got smaller in high school. Free time was rare, since we played sports as much as possible. But as I got older and found more freedom, I naturally headed toward outdoor activities. My mother's family was very involved in the outdoors, both as farmers and as small-game hunters. Rabbits and squirrels were typically the targets, but hard work got in the way of much free time.

That hard work involved being outdoors, though, so without even the thought of hunting or fishing, here I was, outside, in the middle of God's playground, just scratching the surface. Days spent working in a potato field, or shucking corn in the back of my Pa's old Toyota pickup, shaped my appreciation of what the outdoors offered. Stories I heard about my mother's childhood and my grandfathers' childhoods at the farm still live in my head, as alive today as they were when they happened.

The men in my dad's family were serious hunters and fishermen. I grew up seeing them not only duck hunting but also fishing for smallmouth in the rivers, trout in the streams, and catfish in the lakes. Again, I wasn't totally bought in to anything, but I was exposed to yet another aspect of the natural playground. From a young age, little booby traps were being set in my head, just waiting for the right incident to set them off.

After high school, I attended North Carolina State University, where I studied poultry science and worked part-time at a golf course. My classmates were all country boys with similar interests, and my job kept me outside, so the explosives in these booby traps were getting heavier and heavier. It was just a matter of time.

While I was in college, I dated a few young ladies, but one in particular seemed better than any other girl I had ever met. I wasn't sure what it was, but I knew it was something. After years of dating, meeting her family and friends, and seeing how well we went together, I asked her to marry me. Once we made it that far, I moved to where she lived, as she was still in nursing school at East Carolina University.

So, suddenly there I was, in the eastern part of the state. As a western NC boy, this was like moving to a foreign land. I was used to seeing mountain streams full of trout, hunting the ridges for deer, and pursuing the occasional mallard or goose on a lake if the weather was right. Now, I was living in an entirely different section of the playground, one that had blackwater swamps full of wood ducks, coastal creeks with speckled trout, and huge agricultural fields full of roaming whitetails.

To top it all off, the men in my wife's family were all born and bred outdoorsmen. Her dad hunted deer and turkey, and spent his free time all over the country chasing animals. Her older brother was a waterfowler and her younger brother would hunt and fish for anything that moved. Through sheer luck, I landed in a family of guys who would grow to be not only close relatives, but true friends and people I would see, speak to, and hunt with nearly every day of my future life.

This relationship was the trip line that set off all the booby traps in my head. I was no longer someone who happened to be passing through the woods as a spectator. I was addicted to every aspect of the outdoors: the preparation in the offseason, the gear, the locations, and even the new friendships. This obsession, as almost any, can become a burden on relationships if it is allowed to. Your life has to stay balanced, but it is difficult to control your urges to be in the woods every day, especially as a new addict. The temptation is always present, and learning to manage the work/life/hunting balance is something that takes some time.

I've found that as an outdoorsman and a married man, you have to learn the art and style of time management. Your golf friends will still be your friends, but the weekend trips out of town have to take a bit of a back seat. A "kitchen pass" is what a lot of men refer to as an agreed-upon opportunity to leave your home, and the responsibilities that go along with it, to go on a hunting, fishing, or golf trip. Those kitchen passes are valuable and sacred, and for me, they are saved for weekends at the duck club. And who would pass up a weekend at the fishing camp for a concert in Charlotte? I have my allotted time for my hobbies, and all of my hobbies involve being outdoors.

CHAPTER 3

Friendships Forged Through the Outdoors

The network of friends a man puts together as a waterfowler is something that cannot be explained to those who aren't outdoorsmen. I speak to this from the waterfowl perspective because that is how I truly characterize myself. I enjoy all the nuances of hunting and fishing, but waterfowl hunting is what lights that fire of passion to my core.

So, you have your close friends, your brothers-in-law, your friends you grew up with who enjoy the outdoors, and other family members, like uncles and cousins: these people you already had a connection with, and your common love for the outdoors only cements that bond.

Well, then the train goes off the track and you end up with friends you've met along the way but in some cases can't even remember how or where or when.

One of my brother-in-law's best friends has become practically like family to me. He even called me up a few seasons ago to take my son on a youth day hunt. It was a day we'll never forget, as we had thousands of bluebills in the decoys all morning. My son thought we had been holding out this "diver hunting" thing from him. He had no idea that the point we decided to hunt just so happened to be where every scaup and scoter on the north side of the river wanted to be as well.

The final shot of his limit that morning was a drake bluebill from about 40 yards, and my buddy and I can be heard on the video screaming with the joy you only get from moments like this. That drake bluebill is mounted in my son's room to commemorate that day. This friend owed me nothing; this wasn't his way of returning some favor. He had hunted with my son a few days that season, and he really wanted to take him on a youth day—a day away from his own family to be spent with mine, as a true friend would, weaving a strand of the web.

• • •

Some of my closest relationships are with friends who came from my wife's connections. When she began her arduous journey through anesthesia school, one of her twelve classmates was a big duck hunter. His wife and my wife got along, so we started spending time together. Now, ten years later, we are neighbors, friends, and he and I are constant hunting buddies. I get to enjoy seeing his children grow and see him accomplish things in his personal life year-round.

On another occasion, shortly after we were married, we were invited to the wedding of one of my wife's sorority sisters on the Outer Banks of NC. It was going to be a long weekend, and I knew several of the guys who were going, but the day before we left, my wife made a good connection for me. A friend's new boyfriend loved to duck hunt, and since it was a September wedding, he and I decided to teal hunt the Currituck. Two days later, I was on a duck boat with a total stranger, fighting off mosquitoes and swapping hunting tales.

Now, twelve years later, I talk to the guy weekly, hunt with him every year, and feel as close to him as any friend I've ever had. I have even befriended many of his friends from all over the state, and stay in touch with them year-round. About five years ago, one of his friends was litigating a case in my city, and he figured he would reach out and see if we could get together. By happenstance, it was April, so when he called, I asked "You wanna go turkey hunting instead of lunch?" This led to a great afternoon hunt and some great bonding time.

Connections like these are special, and they never seem to stop coming. Next thing you know, you are meeting friends of friends from all over, and now you look at pictures from hunting seasons ten years ago versus today, and there is an entire new fraternity of men you are with. It is one of the most special pieces of the outdoors community.

As you grow with this group, new people are added, and you realize that everyone you meet in this community is connected somehow. You might go to a friend's hunt club and meet with those club members, and without a single exception, you will know some of the same people. I guess birds of a feather truly do flock together.

As I grow older, these friends become far more than just "hunting and fishing buddies." I have spent time in the duck blind with their children, seeing them shoot their first duck. I have had dinner with their families, or we have even vacationed together. I care about their well-being and love their children as if they were my own. It truly has made my life more complete, randomly being put in a position to share time and experiences with these people. I say randomly in jest, as I know this is not the case. In Proverbs 19:21, the Bible says that God's purpose will prevail and that He is in control of even the most random event. There is no way I could believe that a higher power hasn't blessed me with the relationships I have been blessed with.

In fact, I just got off the phone with a former volunteer coordi-nator from Ducks Unlimited that I worked with years ago. Through our relationship, his daughter became my son's babysitter for five years. We all still stay in touch, and I love that family like my own. Our lives were so intertwined for years that we now are all so close. I enjoy keeping up with our former babysitter's new family, and I love to hear my friend's stories about the time he spends with his new grandchildren. This relationship was not an accident.

• • •

Some of my favorite stories to tell happened with some of my great-est friends outdoors doing what we love. A few years ago, when we had some issues with scheduling, several attendees to our annual Ocracoke duck hunting trip wouldn't be able to make it, so a friend and I decided to bring our sons. My son was eleven, and his was eight. We had great aspirations, but getting kids to shoot ducks out of a curtain blind is no easy task. To top it all off, the weather was garbage, warm and foggy every day, so our opportunities were limited. On the second day, the fog was so thick we couldn't even see the farthest decoys. We wanted to hold out hope for a pintail or a redhead on the reef, but realistically, we needed to switch gears so the boys could get some action.

I called the guide, and he had a plan. He had an old stake blind near some oyster beds that was holding about 100 buffleheads. As most duck hunters know, the old buffy isn't top of the list on what you want to chase. Regardless of how beautiful they are, they rarely decoy, typically skirt the spread, and just aren't in the upper pantheon of desired waterfowl targets. They aren't much as table fare, and any enjoyment we might receive from them is often overlooked as we search for other, more exciting species in the area. What I will say now, though, is that hunting a spot loaded with buffleheads may be about as much fun as anything you can do on a slow day. We had flocks of forty and more that would literally appear out of the fog and light right in front of our blind.

We shot three and a half limits that afternoon, but that half limit is my favorite part of the story. My son was experienced enough that he was able to wingshoot and kill several on the fly. My friend's son, on the other hand, was super green. He still needed to shoot them on the water if possible, which is never easy to do in a blind with 40-inch-high walls.

Finally, we moved him to the outside of the blind, on the platform. He sat as still as he could and waited. The fog was to our advantage, as the ducks had just as much trouble seeing us as we had seeing them. After a long wait, a hen landed right in the pocket, and he smoked it. The grin on that boy's face was even wider than ear to ear. But to bust him up even further, a pair came in and landed in the same spot just five minutes later. By God's grace, when he shot this time, they both rolled over dead as a hammer. Those were his first three ducks, in such a special place and with two best friends and their sons hunting together. It just doesn't get much better than that.

• • •

A good old eastern NC swan hunt is always something special, and it also tends be a really fun social event. I have experienced some great hunts all over the eastern part of the state chasing these big white birds. Most of the time, success is inevitable as they are not only large targets, but also not very decoy shy.

Several years ago, I had gotten lucky enough that my hunt party was drawn for our swan tags, and we were able to schedule a hunt on a perfect Saturday morning. I headed out with the guide along with my dad, my uncle, and my cousin to the never-ending wheat fields around Pungo Lake, where we hid in a ditch. Decoys were out, and in no time, we had giant birds all over us. My dad has a lot of factors against him when it comes to wingshooting. He has brittle bone disease, and has broken more bones than you can imagine. With that, he is often sore or out of sorts, and shouldering a 12-gauge isn't always the easiest. On top of that, a stroke several years ago ruined one of his eyes, so he also has terrible depth perception.

One of the first birds to pass by that morning was just out of range. The guide hollered "Don't shoot," but Dad also can't hear very well. He pulled up, got one shot out of the gun, and that bird fell like a sack of potatoes at about 50 yards deep. The look of accomplishment in his face was only topped by the look of shock on my uncle's face at him making that shot.

I shot one right in the hole, as did my uncle a few minutes later. This was not intentional, but now, my cousin, who was fourteen with limited wingshooting practice, was the only member in our party left to shoot. She shot, and she shot, and she shot some more. Her dad, my uncle, was in her ear, maybe making it a little more nerve-racking. I had my little handheld camcorder and just enjoyed the show. I made sure she was aware that we were in no rush, and that she was doing great.

She has always had a great relationship with my dad, which is interesting because I have always had a great relationship with her dad. We seem more comfortable hunting with our uncles sometimes. My dad moved down beside her, and brought her his 12-gauge to try to shoot. All the while, we were in the midst of what would be considered "as good as it gets" in the swan field. The guide knew that opportunities were gonna keep coming, so he reassured her as well. Finally, on her second volley with the 12-gauge, a swan fell and soared across the field. The guide's daughter, who was about sixteen years old and wide open, chased that bird down, tackled it before it got away, and brought it back.

We basked in our glory for quite a while. It was a family moment that couldn't be replicated anywhere else. About ten years later, I was finally able to enjoy this same kind of experience with my son on his first swan hunt. We both shot one, and got to watch as the rest of the hunt party shot theirs, but this time it just wasn't the same. I was proud, and it was fun, but what I would've given to have the rest of the family there to share it.

A few years have passed since that hunt with my cousin, and

I've come to realize that hunting and fishing are the most important things my dad and I have together. We don't always agree on
politics, and we don't have a ton of other common interests. At
any time, though, we can grab a rod or a gun and we are as close
as any two humans can be. This is especially important now, in
his older years, as I want us to be able to spend fun times together
as much as possible, and there's always something to do in the
woods.

• • •

Some of the memories that will last a lifetime are the ones that
were made during hunts that included my kids along with friends
I've only met within the past ten years, but are so close they essentially are like another family. My son shot his first duck on the
wing with one of my buddies on his ponds. I remember thinking
we were going to have to let birds land all day to get my son any
shots, as he was only eight at the time. The first single of the morning came dropping in, but you could tell at the last minute it was
going to get squirrelly and pick up and leave. We told my son to
shoot, and boom, he smoked it right over the decoys. My friend
and I looked at each other and grinned. We knew if he could do
that, we were about to wear them out. Sure enough, he shot his first
limit that day.

One cold, rainy fall day, my buddy from Greensboro was in
town and wanted to run the boat out to the Pungo to see if we
could catch some fish. He knew my son was getting into it big time,

so he wanted to take him and let him be the fish catcher for the day. It was so cold and miserable, my son's lips were blue all day. I'd ask him if he wanted to leave, and he would say, "One more fish." After about twenty "one more fish" answers to that question, we had already missed his baseball practice and I saw no end in sight. My friend wanted to fish all day, and so did my son, so here I was, just making sure everyone had snacks. We caught so many fish that I lost count. Trout, flounder, puppy drum by the boat load. To this day, my son recalls this as his best day of fishing ever, and I can't argue that at all. My friend knew what he was doing, and how to catch them, and he knew how to make my son feel special.

Fast-forward to a few years later, running and gunning for turkeys in the woods with my son and his "Uncle Twig." Twig is a friend I met through mutual connections a long time ago. He is a true man of the woods and a great handyman. In fact, the first time I met him, our mutual friend had sent him to my house to help install a new hot water heater. Instantly, we hit it off and have been friends ever since.

My son tried turkey hunting from a blind with decoys for a while, but it just never got him excited. Sitting in one spot and hoping for a turkey to show up can be challenging for someone who is easily subject to boredom, such as a young boy. Finally, one youth season, Twig wanted to tag along and take my son running and gunning through the woods. We heard gobbles, and we worked toward them and stayed on it. This method was unsuccessful the first two years we tried it, but my son fell in love with it. You see, my friend is not only one of the best turkey hunters I know, but also very patient with kids, and truth be told, he's mostly still a kid himself. Finally, during year three, our efforts came to fruition.

At first light, we had heard two separate gobblers near the back food plot. In an effort to put ourselves somewhere between the two, we made a plan and set up in the middle of the plot to patiently wait. As the sun got high enough to cast a long shadow across the plot, I saw the gobbler in the back corner. He strutted and gobbled all the way across the plot, seemingly about to walk all the way to our laps. Unfortunately, though, somewhere at about 50 yards, he had a change of heart. I don't know if he saw us, or maybe just didn't like something with the decoys, but either way, we had to watch him slowly walk away. My son was confused, and slightly disappointed, but Twig quickly reminded us of the other bird, which was still gobbling.

We shifted gears and set up for a rear-approaching bird. I had to relieve myself, so I took a few steps back in the woods. Twig and I were discussing our plan before I sat back down. Then in mid-sentence, Twig's eyes got huge, and he grabbed my arm. The other gobbler was coming in from the left, strutting into the decoy as if on a string.

I tried to get my son's attention quietly, but luckily he was already on point. As the bird strutted into range at 15 yards, he easily raised his gun and made a great shot. He had finally got his bird without a blind. Quite the accomplishment, and Twig was quite the friend to put in that much effort to allow it to happen. To this day, every youth season is met with the question, "Is Twig coming with us?"

My son got to experience another first this year, as he was invited to tag along on an out-of-state duck hunt. A great group of recent friends decided to make a trip to Reelfoot Lake for a three-day hunt. Most of the crew was flying in to Memphis, but I am a road trip man at heart. Luckily, another member of the crew also loved a good road trip, so we decided to run it together. We knew each other well enough. We had hunted together several times and had seen each other at social gatherings. With that said, nothing can prepare a relationship to either blow up or jell permanently more than fourteen consecutive hours in a truck together. My son was with us as well, and he did great. No complaining, mostly just sleeping and listening, with the occasional comment. But my friend and I grew our friendship by ten years on that ride. We talked about family, friends, and life experiences. I am so happy we decided to make that ride together, because it built something that would never have been built otherwise. Another close friend came from the love of a duck.

• • •

The most powerful examples of how these friendships grow has been seen through my oldest relationships. My best friend, whose name became my son's middle name, got back into hunting around the time we both were getting married. We don't live near one another, but through our annual hunt trips and our lake trips in the summer, we see each other as often as possible. If we hadn't gone on these duck hunting trips over the past fifteen years, or weren't still telling the stories of those trips, I don't know where our relationship would be. Our kids think we are brothers, and our wives are great friends. All our children act as if they're siblings, and I cannot help but think that this is totally attributed to our common love of the outdoors.

Another great friend from my hometown has always been an outdoorsman. We lived in a college fraternity house together, and built a strong relationship. At one point, years passed without us seeing one another. Life pulled us in different directions, but the wonder of wildlife pulled us back together. One spring morning about twenty years ago, we were both in town to see our families. He called me, and we planned to meet at Little Fisher River on opening day of trout season. Immediately, we picked up right where we had left off. Since then, not a season passes without us getting together. Every out-of-state duck trip I've ever been on, he's been there right beside me. Hunts in Ocracoke, turkey hunts in Northampton, and all else in between. Our sons are now coming along on these trips, and seeing them spend time together is icing on the cake.

• • •

I have a particular group of friends that has been tight-knit since high school. I live across the state from these guys, but we stay in touch a lot. In the past five years, we discovered that one thing we could all agree on was a love for fishing. Whenever we could, we would plan around our busy schedules to go fishing for smallmouth or trout.

Recently, one of those friends unexpectedly passed away. Initially I was very sad, and I still am, to be honest. I would love to have one more conversation with him. But, when I really reflect, I praise God for the fishing trips we had. That was the only way we all made time for one another, and I am so thankful. And where would these relationships be without a common passion for the outdoors? Again, there are no coincidences in this world. I am sure of that. I am, once again, a lucky man.

CHAPTER 4

Hunting and Fishing Spots

Some of the most special places on earth are the public wildlife areas, hunting and fishing clubs, or leases that a person will visit in their lifetime. A few years back I started dropping a pin on my Google Maps app so later on I could see where I had been. Quickly, though, I realized that it was a futile effort for maintaining a memory. I can go look at the pins all I want, but they don't relay

10 percent of the info that my brain recalls when I think of the location.

Special "spots," especially on public land, are often a source of serious conflict and privacy. I have started to ease away from public hunting as much as I possibly can in the past few years, mainly due to some of the confrontations I have witnessed in the past. The stories of fights over hunting spots on Pamlico Sound, and some of the rude encounters I've had with folks setting up less than 100 yards away, were too much for me.

With that said, I will add that I have been a part of some magnificent hunts and have seen some of the most beautiful places the Lord has designed on a piece of federal- or state-owned public land. I've shot a three-man limit of wigeon on a little state-maintained saltwater impoundment with two buddies. We were three young twenty-somethings who accidentally applied for the wrong impoundment and won, and then got really lucky. We stumbled in that morning, threw out some decoys, and had that three-man limit in thirty minutes. We would have flocks of forty to fifty wigeon work right over the trees, coming from the river, and try to sit in our laps. I am not sure that any of us had experienced many sights like that at that point in our lives. We had no idea what we were getting into, and we were surprised at how amazing that spot was.

I've seen another state-run spot that had a variety of grain and natural vegetation impoundments absolutely full of ringnecks and pintails. Back in the day, when there weren't hunt locations assigned, and you would have to race on the dike at 4 a.m. for your spot. Having some fleet-footed friends and a good scout could put you in a hole as good as any in the state. These areas can offer great opportunities for hunters who lack access to private spots for a productive hunt, and they can definitely be worth the trip.

Of course, private land can also be a source of some "secret" spots that can cause some conflict. Someone may have their own spot where they are running a camera and hunting a certain deer, or they may have a secret, out-of-the-way swamp hole where they know there will be some ducks. That's just the nature of the beast to certain folks, but my approach has always been different. My mindset has always been that if you have access to a special place, share it with as many of your people as you can. Honestly, I have been awarded many amazing places to set my lucky feet on thanks to friendships I have made. Some of the most memorable hunts and fishing trips I have been a part of have been on other people's property as an invited guest.

One such hunt occurred on Christmas Eve 2024, when my son, my father, and I were invited to go to a friend's duck impoundment. It was a new property that he had busted his tail on to make perfect, and since it was finally looking the way he envisioned it, he wanted to share it. Unfortunately my dad could not attend, as he was sick, but my son and I made it happen. What we witnessed with three other friends was a spectacle of waterfowl most folks will never see in a small duck hole. Hundreds of birds of all varieties piled in there, to the point that we didn't even shoot; we just watched in awe. As soon as the birds broke the tree line over the corner of the property, they were gliding and backpedaling in our faces in every direction. Another mule kick to the chest. At one point in the morning, I suggested that we get ready, as we were "about to have to shoot in self-defense." We shot wood ducks, mallards, gadwall, and teal. To top it off, my son shot his first limit as one of the "dudes" that morning. Yet despite how great the shooting and my son's accomplishment had been, the best part was still the show we got at first light.

Enjoying those opportunities makes me even more excited when I get to share some of those experiences from my own hunting spots with others. Luckily for me, my friend group all seems to have that same approach. I have friends who are members of some of the finest hunting clubs and establishments in the state, and I cannot begin to tell you how grateful I am to get to see those places and experience the history as a mere speck of dust on their memory boards.

The renowned Neupamba Duck Club comes to mind, a place second to none in North Carolina, which has hosted all sorts of guests. The camaraderie amongst the members, the blessings over the meals, the treatment of the guests, and the unbelievable duck hunts are something I am so lucky to be a part of. Sitting in a blind with your friends, getting to hear the wigeon and pintails whistling in the wind as they pour in off the sound, shooting some of the most beautiful birds eastern NC has to offer, and then celebrating it with the rest of the club afterward is what hunting is all about. This club identifies with my values as much as any place I have been. It has the meals, the great hunting, the junk talking amongst friends, and most important, the fellowship that is so important to the health and enjoyment of a duck camp.

One cold, December Thursday, the friend who is a member at Neupamba called me to ask if I wanted to join him for a hunt there the following day. These opportunities are never something to pass up, but being that my wife works in the hospital, she is typically gone early every morning. My role during the week includes getting the kids up and ready for school and then dropping them off.

On such short notice, I knew this was going to be a challenge, but I had a little extra gas on my fire about this. After several phone calls and some next-day preparation, I had the plans for the kids taken care of. I loaded up all of my gear and headed out with excitement pulsing through my veins.

I arrived just in time for dinner. I knew many of the members already, but there were a few new guests I was fortunate enough to meet. We shared stories over dinner, talked plans for the following day, then got in bed to get some rest for the next day.

The conditions were perfect. Cold temperatures, a strong north wind, and we had reports that there were lots of birds using the property. I barely slept, and woke up well before my alarm went off. After some coffee and some early morning junk talk, blinds were drawn. We drew a blind that had not been hunted all year, so we were somewhat unsure of how the hunt would play out. Another friend was also invited, so we had all three of us loading up the boat and heading out in no time. The ride out was bitterly cold, but the anticipation of what the morning held kept us plenty warm through the biting winds.

We arrived at our blind with plenty of time to set out the

decoys with methodical precision. Then we hopped into the blind to watch the pre-light show of ducks coming in. The spectacle that takes place on this property in the minutes leading up to legal shooting time never disappoints. Wigeon and pintail were pouring in off the sound in huge groups. Any concerns we had about how successful this blind was going to be were quickly erased. Even over the gusting winds, the air was filled with the sounds of wigeon whistling and wings flapping. We seemed to have an unlimited supply of ducks eager to mingle with our decoys, providing not only easy shots, but also awe-inspiring sights.

As shooting time arrived, we all loaded our guns to prepare for the hunt. In no time, we were shooting at group after group working our decoy spread just as we had hoped. We carefully picked out drakes, and quickly began to fill out limit with wigeons and pintails. As the morning hunt came to an end, we ended with a stud drake black duck and a gorgeous drake blue-winged teal.

The only unfortunate thing about a hunt like this is that it is usually over too quickly. As much as I enjoy the shooting, seeing the beauty of the birds working is hard to leave. In no time, we had the decoys picked up and the gear packed, and we were back at the house by 8:30 a.m. We cooked up hash browns, bacon, and eggs for the rest of the group, and once everyone arrived back to camp, we all sat down for a welcomed meal. Stories of the morning were shared around the table as the warm breakfast and hot coffee helped everyone shake the chill of the morning.

To this day, this experience is often what I think of when this place is discussed. I have been lucky enough to spend some work weekends down there, and several other hunts, but this quick trip cemented the legacy of that place in my brain. And to make it even better, I was still able to be home in time to pick the kids up from school.

• • •

I have also been blessed to be a part of the famed and ancient Camp Bryan. Babe Ruth and Ted Williams graced this property, and now little old me gets to enjoy the same experiences. I have seen bears killed there, shot two turkeys, and had some unbelievable duck hunts on the amazing Lake Ellis-Simon. Meeting the members and hearing some of their old stories, then getting to see it myself is something that can't be duplicated. I have even been able to share a few of these experiences with my son, so I understand what a lucky man I am.

My favorite duck hunt ever took place on this lake, where six close friends and I shot a seven-man limit of puddle ducks in what can only be described as an epic hunt. Perfect weather, perfect location, and great shooting. We even initially set up incorrectly, with the sun directly in our faces. After we reconfigured our setup and got comfortable, we had every species of puddle duck in NC show off for us for the next three hours. It was cold, clear, and windy. We were hiding in the shade of the big cypress trees covered in Spanish moss, totally unseen by any of the birds. With the sun in the ducks' eyes and to our backs, and a stiff 15 mph breeze, it was, for once, like shooting fish in a barrel.

The hunt party was larger than we had hunted out there before, so we had five hunting in the boat blind, while another friend and I stood in the water at the bow of the boat, nestled under some low-hanging cypress branches. The action was almost overwhelming at times. We tried to communicate what we saw, but there were times when it seemed as if we were in a bee hive, with ducks buzzing in every direction.

Flocks of more than fifty teal came in and humbled us with their ability to dodge the gunfire. Gadwalls worked beautifully, and the always reliable ringnecks put on a show. This lake is known for its ringneck population, and seeing those birds fly in at full speed with the wind cutting their wings so hard they sound as if a fighter jet is approaching is incomparable. Lots of other varieties made appearances, including a pair of pintails that managed to sneak out unscathed.

A friend shot his first mallard that morning, and we shot a bag with seven species of ducks. I can still see the way the sun peeked through the moss hanging from the cypress trees over my shoulder, and the mid-morning stud black duck that crept right through our decoys as we were picking up. As the hunt ended, I walked about 150 yards away from the setup to pick up a drake wood duck I had sailed earlier in the hunt. As I picked it up, I turned around to see six grown men smiling so big you could see their gums in the sunshine. I paused a minute, while catching my breath from the walk, to enjoy this sight. It's yet another example of an experience that can only happen in the pursuit of wildlife.

• • •

Hyde County and Lake Mattamuskeet are legendary staples of waterfowling in NC, and hunting the surrounding private impoundments and the federal blinds on the lake is another experience I have enjoyed. Hunting the sink boxes on the Outer Banks is something else only NC can offer. I have enjoyed many hunting trips with a guide in Ocracoke, which is a part of Hyde County that many people overlook because it is so disconnected from the rest of the county. Over the years we have become close with this guide, keeping in touch year-round. We fish with him in the summer, catching all grades of trout and drum. We have hunted with his family for over twelve years, and have had some hunts there that you would never believe. There have been days when you couldn't move your head without seeing a pintail.

In 2019 a huge freeze covered the state, and even a significant part of the Pamlico Sound was frozen. Our trip to hunt in the stake blinds just so happened to be scheduled on the first day of the thaw. What we saw that first day may never be duplicated. We had fifty thousand redheads flying low and decoying all day long. We simply started filming, as we had our limits, but just couldn't leave the show we were watching. The guide we use down there is a young kid, second generation, but he is as close as a brother to me. He is always checking in on my son and his adventures. Last year, he even carved an amazing wigeon for my son that we gave him as a gift. It was a dead-mount carving, and we mounted my son's first wigeon as a dead mount right beside it, on the same board. That may be one of the coolest pieces of duck art a man could ever see, and is yet another example of the ever-growing web of friendships formed in this endeavor.

• • •

There are so many fond memories from small, private pieces of land that I have hunted on with family and friends that I could never recount them all. One fall morning I was there to witness a good friend shoot an old eleven-point buck on his family farm in Northampton County. We had gotten up to a cold November morning, made colder by the fact that the wood stove in the cabin had gone out overnight. We chugged some coffee to warm up our insides before we headed to the stand. He had his sights on this buck, but we were just having a good time and trying to see what would happen. Not ten minutes after sunrise I heard the shot, and ran over there to see the buck lying right in his tracks and my buddy smiling like a mule eating briars. This was no Boone and Crockett, but this was a trophy for us.

Several of my friends have small clubs and leases all over the state. Some of my most memorable duck hunts took place in a little club in Pamlico County, back before we all had children. We would duck hunt all day long, and see things that the average duck hunter, who picks up at 9 a.m., would never witness. I've seen everything from a hundred bluebills falling out of the sky into a small impoundment at 3 p.m. to my first-ever pintail drake on a cold December morning.

That last is particularly meaningful because a pintail drake had been my benchmark of a trophy bird since I was a child. I remember that my grandfather had an old, ratty pintail mount in his living room, among several other birds. Regardless of the quality of this taxidermy, the beauty of the pintail was obvious. Once I really started duck hunting seriously, the pintail was my goal.

For years I had done everything I could to put myself in the right situation to shoot one of those birds, but it began to feel like it would never happen. By this point, I had accepted my fate and decided that I would just have to be ready whenever the opportunity arose, but I wasn't going to allow myself to obsess over it anymore.

The evening before this hunt changed that perspective entirely. When we climbed into the observation tower to scout the impoundment, we could see hundreds of pintails sitting together, right in front of the blind we were going to hunt. Anticipation was high and I could barely fall asleep that night.

The next morning, our group headed out to the makeshift blind and set out the decoys. The three guys with me were all great friends, and we had hunted together many times before. We knew our role, and got the decoys set out and the gear set up in record time. As we sat there, watching the sky and awaiting the early flight of birds, one of my friends spoke up and said, "The first pintail drake that comes in this morning, no one else but John can shoot.

The first one is his." Wow, no pressure there, huh? I loaded my gun and awaited the arrival of my bird. Sure enough, as soon as the clock hit shooting time, here came a beautiful drake pintail, back-pedaling into our decoy spread at 10 yards.

I immediately stood up and fired. BOOM! I missed, but here came shot number two. BOOM! Missed again. Now my nerves had turned to steel, and my determination took over. On the third shot, he was still well within range. I took my time and BOOM! He folded into the decoys belly up, almost at our feet. When the dog returned my prize, I wanted to take a minute to really soak in the moment. There was no time, though. We were in the middle of what would end up being one of the best hunts this place ever produced.

We patiently waited to fill our pintail limit before shooting at any other species. Gadwall were falling in by the hundreds, but the pintails were floating just overhead, so we had to be patient. At one point, one of my friends looked at me and said "I don't think I can take this anymore!" Finally we had our pintails, so the other tar-gets were open game. We shot gadwall, green-winged teal, limits of black ducks, and finished the limit on a nice group of ringnecks that came in too close.

That evening, as we were in the camp house, celebrating and cooking dinner, we were all saying goodbye to the friend who had to head back home for the evening. The rest of us were spending the night to go home on Sunday, but he had a new baby and had some dad duties to attend to. This was the friend who had invited me, and the friend who made the pre-light announcement for me to get the shot at the first pintail. I gave him an awkward hug as he left. It wasn't awkward for me, as I am an emotional guy who loves a good hug, but his mood had shifted away from hunt camp and back to home, so he was caught off guard. I thanked him as much as I could, but he would never really know how special that hunt was to me.

Years later, during another hunt at this club, we had scouted the day before and saw practically no ducks. That previous evening, I had seen only five ringnecks in the whole impoundment, and I barely saw anything flying the creek at sunset. We knew that historically the area held ducks, and we had great weather moving in the next day. Still, we just decided to build a blind where those five ducks had been and give it a shot. To our surprise, we were lucky enough to be sitting in the flyway of this area during a migration. Fresh birds showed up all day. We shot wigeon, teal, gadwall, and some ringnecks. We shot a three-man limit just after lunch, and after what I had seen the day before, I would say that was one of the more unbelievable accomplishments in my duck hunting career.

• • •

Although I have enjoyed all the experiences I have had on private hunting clubs with my friends, I must admit that the family farm in Northampton County holds the most significant place in my heart. Since I moved to eastern NC, I have spent every hunting season chasing something up there. When I first started, it was covered in eight- to ten-year-old pines with a super-thick understory. It was a great spot for rabbits, and there were plenty of deer on the property. You mainly had to hunt paths, but it was still a pretty active spot. A few years later, a logging crew came out and cleared out a good section of the cypress swamp. This resulted in some serious wood duck action for a few years in the little potholes that resulted from fallen trees and overturned root balls.

Over the years, the pines have grown, the cutover in the swamp has filled in, and the property has developed into a great, diverse landscape that is prime-time for wildlife. When the property was thinned a few years back, we created some food plots. In the past ten years we have added some awesome tower stands, built multiple duck blinds, cleared holes in the swamp, controlled vegetation in the summer, planted duck food in the fall, and stocked the pond with fish.

Today, this place produces healthy wildlife year-round. The fishing is great, turkeys are plentiful, deer numbers and quality are improving, and the swamp continues to provide steady, solid hunts every year. The culmination of all of our work is that we now have such a special place to share with family and friends. The memories here are stored in a photo album in the cabin, and it is really impressive to see the photos from the past fifteen-plus years.

As I mentioned earlier, my son shot his first deer, duck, and turkey here, and I too shot my first turkey on this farm. As a fairly green turkey hunter, my first several seasons were marred by close calls and missed shots. Turkey hunting is a challenge, and lessons are learned daily. Even then, being able to finish the job and shoot the bird is no easy task.

I had never turkey hunted this property, but my father-in-law urged me to give it a try, as he thought there might be some birds roosting somewhere near the cabin along the swamp. I decided it was worth taking the chance, so I headed to the farm, parked at the gate so I'd be far away from where I might spook any roosted birds, and walked down to the cabin.

Once I arrived, I realized that I hadn't really made any plans further than this. I had no idea what to expect, so I just sat on the porch swing and waited for a gobbling tom to announce his location. As the sun began to come up, the sound of gobbles nearly blew me off the porch. I don't know what I expected, but it definitely wasn't this. Several birds sounded off, no more that 50 to 100 yards away, just by the cabin. Where do I go? How do I set up? What is even happening? These thoughts all raced through my head as I clumsily hopped off the porch and hid against the wall farthest from where the birds were. I knew if I moved anywhere else in the open, I'd be spotted. So, my genius idea was to just stand there, wait for them to fly down, then somehow come up with another plan.

As I stood there in a stupor, another bird started gobbling from another direction. I paused to listen, and sure enough this bird was already on the ground. He was coming down the path, or so it seemed, coming from my side of the cabin. Now I was in the wide open from his point of view, so it was time for my fast-acting brain to come up with Plan B.

At that time, we had only a small storage barn with a lean-to beside the cabin. Under the lean-to were all of our tractor implements, including a big, orange Bush Hog. I belly-crawled to it, hiding behind the low-profile equipment as low as I could. When I raised my head up a little and peeked out, there he was, walking straight toward me, gobbling every other breath. I ducked back down and waited. His next gobble gave his location away, and I knew he was in range. I got my gun ready and eased up, ready to shoot. Luckily, he never expected any danger behind the equipment, and I was able to make a perfect shot at 15 yards. I relive this moment every time I stand in the yard of the cabin. It was definitely one of the more unique turkey hunts I've ever experienced.

We have spent family Christmases in the cabin, celebrated birthdays, hosted friends and family, and made thousands of family memories sitting on this piece of land. We hid here for weeks during quarantine, and I can remember the entire family sitting around watching my then two-year-old daughter dance and sing church songs while we all laughed and sang along. We built gingerbread houses on the porch a few Christmas Eves ago, when we stayed up there because it was close to the hospital where my wife was working that weekend. The boys and girls of the family have caught countless bass in the pond, and many a meal has been cooked on the little Weber on the porch.

On the final youth day of duck season a few years ago, my two brothers-in-law took my son and my youngest nephew into a blind, hopeful that would we could cap off a slow season with a bang. You see, that entire season had been ruined by a poacher. For nearly the entire season, there was a young man from out of town who frequented our property during the week, conveniently while we were not there. It took us nearly the entire season to catch him, and when we finally did, we learned the extent of this violation. It turned out that he had been taking his kayak in there all year, as he seemed to think this was public property. He had even hunted from our blinds and shot countless birds. On the final day of the season, we caught the trespasser on the property ourselves. We were able to get the game warden involved, and without any charges being filed, the intruder was made fully aware of his wrongdoing and has not returned since.

We took it on the chin that year, but we still wanted the boys to get one good hunt in there to try to save the season. We had scouted the night before, and didn't see much, but we hoped we could still shoot something cool, or get my youngest nephew his first duck. The morning started off slowly, seeing hardly any first-light wood ducks and almost zero other ducks flying around. The boys were having fun with one another, so spirits were still high, but realistically I was getting ready to walk out of this swamp empty-handed for what would not have been the first time that season.

Just then, though, right as the sun popped over through the tall cypresses to our right, we saw three ducks working down the swamp. Immediately, I could tell what they were. Only three days prior, I had returned from a duck hunting trip to the Laguna Madre in Mexico, and I saw enough pintails in those several days to satisfy a lifetime. When I looked up, there was no doubt that we had two drakes and a hen pintail coming right into our hole.

The boys jumped up, and my son knocked one down right in the hole. My brother-in-law, in his youthful excitement, ran across the swamp like an Olympic sprinter. When he brought it back to the blind, the boys laid the bull sprig across the cypress branches that were placed along the front of the blind to brush it in. I do not know if I can ever say that I have seen a more beautiful pintail, and we all basked in that beauty the rest of the morning. From bill to long tail, he was perfect. We didn't shoot another bird that morning, but not a soul cared. We were all happy as a pig in slop walking back to the truck that morning, with a magnificent specimen of a bull sprig in our possession. As of this day, that is the only pintail ever harvested on the farm. What a memory it created, and what a great way that was to rescue a season of struggles. There are very few places on this planet that hold a place in my heart as special as this piece of property does.

• • •

My son's first racked buck was on a little lease we had in Edge-combe County. We would fish the pond, shoot turkeys, and even shoot a few early season ducks in there. I haven't stepped foot there in years, but I can still smell the swamp and hear the hum of the cotton gin in the background from where we would deer hunt. This small piece of land holds such significance for us, as this was a farm that my father-in-law had grown up hunting when he was a young man. Seeing his grandchildren hunting out there was very special, I am sure. Not only did my son shoot that first buck there; my nephew shot his first deer there as well. This farm offered so much variety of wildlife and habitats. My son was able to spend a lot of his early days out there before we lost the lease, and he still remembers several specifics and stories about the property.

I also once leased a small piece of property just outside of the town where I live now. It was wildly underutilized, but I have some amazing memories from that place that cement it in my mind forever. One December weekend, years ago, my uncle and my best friend were in town for a public impoundment hunt we were drawn for. My uncle arrived early, so we decided to spend some time riding out to the lease and investigating. I had just restored an old johnboat a friend had given me. I wanted to take it out to the property and find a good spot to leave it where it could be used. As we walked the long path that runs through the middle of the swamp, we stumbled upon a hole, marked by one of the largest cypress trees I have ever seen. It was holding a pile of birds. Our plans then adjusted, as we planned to see what we could do there.

The next day brought not only unbelievable hunting but also some memorable moments. We shot mallards and wood ducks galore; in a morning marred by low-hanging fog, the ducks couldn't avoid us when they flew by. We made a five-course breakfast in the johnboat floating in the bush, I saw my best friend shoot back-to-back doubles that would impress John Wayne, and my uncle fell into the swamp face-first in slow motion while my friend and I were shooting a three-pack of mallards floating in. This was the only successful duck hunt I ever had on this lease, but it was a special one with great company. Every duck season, I catch myself wondering if there are any birds in that hole. In my mind I can still see that giant cypress holding court over one of the most serene swamp holes I've ever been in.

I even spent a season hunting a small pond on the side of the highway that a few guys and I leased. We had some of the most epic ringneck shoots you could imagine, right off that busy road, just outside of town. We had hunted this pond for years, but were restricted to using it after deer season only. That year, though, we paid the landowner a fee to use it all season. By the grace of God, that was the most productive season we ever had there. We shot ringnecks and some mixed-in gadwall and redheads from Thanksgiving through the end of the season. We built some dog-wire blinds on each side of the pond, allowing us to hunt any wind, and I kept my kayak up there all year. This allowed me to retrieve ducks if we didn't have a dog, and to put out decoys on the deep end of the pond when we had a north wind.

I once shot two banded redheads there in one hunt. My friend and I were huddled on the bank as two drakes came flying in. We shot the birds on our sides, mine on the left, his on the right. As his dog returned them, I saw that mine was banded. It was my first ever. Then, not ten minutes later, the exact same scenario happened. Once again, the one I shot was banded. Amazingly enough, they were both banded by the same man, in the same spot in Lake Manitoba, seven years apart. What are the odds of that happening?

· · ·

The farm where I grew up holds a special place in my heart, and I have a lifetime of memories from there. When I was a kid, seeing a deer in the woods on our property was along the lines of seeing Sasquatch. We hunted hard, built stands, and would maybe see a few every year, and ideally kill one. Wild turkeys were literally nowhere to be found on this farm. Although I was very young at the time—I couldn't have been more than six or seven—I do remember that the state was running a program in which they were relocating wild turkeys to farms all over in hopes that the population would spread and grow. My uncle and dad signed up, and I remember that we had three jakes and four hens held up in the old pig sty behind my grandparents' house. We were going to throw the turkeys in the enclosed trailer that night, when they were calm, and carry them on top of the ridge. I had never seen a wild turkey, so I was very excited to witness this event. My uncle, who on most Saturday nights was usually testing out the whiskey pretty heavily to see how it helped his singing voice, was no less than three sheets to the wind when our project began.

I can see this memory in my head right now as if I were watching it in real time. He stepped into the pen to grab the first turkey, and was met with a pretty aggressive young male that wanted nothing to do with him. For about thirty seconds, a tussle went down that was akin to a fight with the Tasmanian devil in the old cartoons. Dust was flying, feathers were falling, and ultimately, my uncle limped out with his shirt ripped off and his pride lost in a pile of feathers and dirt. With no better option after this incident, those turkeys were just let out of the cage right there behind the houses. As the years passed we never saw or heard them, and that effort slowly became a distant memory.

Fast-forward about fifteen years to a call I received from my dad after a springtime fishing trip to the neighbor's pond. Obviously, he had caught some fish he was excited to tell me about, but most important, he swore that he heard a gobble at first light from the ridge. Sure enough, a population of turkeys had taken hold up there and was beginning to grow in numbers. Over the next five to ten years we would see nice flocks in the fields and at the feeders during deer season. My dad was even lucky enough to shoot his first-ever wild turkey during that time, and right across the road from the house.

Every year, I would assure my dad, "Hey, I'm coming to turkey hunt up there this year, I've got to shoot one on the old family farm!" But between personal scheduling conflicts and youth sports, I never seemed to be able to make it.

Finally, a weekend opportunity presented itself, and I found myself heading to my parents' house in mid-April. Come hell or high water, I was at least gonna try to turkey hunt. That first morning, I woke up extra early and walked up on the ridge. I heard a few gobbles, but having done zero scouting and also having zero idea of how to properly approach hunting turkeys in the foothills, I was unsuccessful.

I came in for lunch and saw that my cousin was there to visit me and my kids. Her husband loves to turkey hunt, and he had been over there two days prior. He said that around 3 p.m., he was set up in the back field when he heard someone stomping through the woods. He was sure there was a trespasser approaching, so he stood up to go meet them, when to his surprise, he instead spooked two gobblers that had been heading right to him. The trees there are all old hardwoods, and the forest floor is 100 percent oak and maple leaves, which are the loudest thing to walk on in the woods, even for a "violator" in the form of a couple of toms.

I took in this intel, saw on my watch that it was around 2 p.m., and decided I needed to see if they would stay on pattern and pull this move again. I got up in the woods, right on the intersection of some old logging roads, and set up. I grew up in these woods, looking for box turtles, riding my Yamaha 100 all through the trails, bringing home jars of tadpoles from the mud puddles, and most recently, deer hunting with my dad. This little chunk of the earth is as much a part of me as my bloodline. The smell, the sound, the holly trees mixed in with the rhododendrons and the hardwoods—this place is so, so special.

I sat at the base of an old busted white oak, and just for entertainment, yelped really loudly on my box call to see if I could get a reaction. To my surprise, a gobble sounded off so close and so loud that I nearly fell over. From the best I could figure, this bird was coming from my left, right down the logging trail.

I was ready, and then, I heard something else. The loud footsteps my cousin had confused with a trespasser were coming right behind me, from left to right. The sound of dead leaves being crunched along the forest floor was to my advantage for once, as I knew where the turkeys were, but at the same time, they were exactly where I couldn't shoot. As a right-handed gunner, I needed the birds to be somewhere between my due left and straight ahead, but somehow, they had meandered all the way around me and seemed to be directly to my right. As I peeked over my right shoulder, I saw two strutting gobblers making a semicircular path headed to my right. As they moved behind a tree, I wiggled into position slowly, then had to make the decision to shoot before they could possibly disappear. As one stuck his head out from behind an old possum pine, I pulled the trigger and smoked him. I had done it. I am not the best turkey hunter by any means; I have probably been lucky enough to harvest a dozen in my days, so this was a great accomplishment. And due to the timing and location, this was my favorite of all time, and probably always will be.

• • •

Although North Carolina has more than enough places to hunt, there also are spots all over the country that hold a special place in my memories. Deer and turkey hunting in central Texas is something all outdoorsmen should experience. Seeing a hundred deer a day in the mesquite plains, while also seeing hordes of other wildlife, is a hunter's dream.

I was once there in a very severe spring storm. This storm dumped as much rain in two days as this area would usually get in an entire year. We were limited on where we could hunt, if we could even get out at all. But early morning cups of coffee in the lodge, watching *Braveheart* at bedtime, and hearing the woods wake up with gobbles in every direction made the challenge worth the while.

Sea duck hunting the coast of Rhode Island and Massachusetts is another one of my favorites. Three of my closest friends and I packed up, drove north, and before we knew it, we were in the ocean shooting ducks we had never seen before. We hunted a spot called Buzzards Bay one day. There had to be over thirty thousand eiders in this area, and we dug a hole in the sand, covered up with painters cloths, and commenced to shooting some of North America's most unique-looking and tough-skinned creatures. We shot eider, old squaw, bluebills, and some scoters as well.

I've seen the huge blinds of Tennessee's Lake Reelfoot, where my son and I, along with a group of friends and their kids, spent three days seeing what that was all about. The hunting wasn't the best, as we were not there at the most opportune time, but the experience was great. Hunting a blind big enough for twelve, with a lounge and a kitchen; eating two meals and drinking fresh coffee and orange juice all day; the kids with us felt like they were in hog heaven.

Along the way I've been fortunate enough to go duck hunting on Laguna Madre in Mexico multiple times. Spending time with friends in a foreign land, shooting boat loads of ducks and quail while eating local cuisine, is an out-of-this-world experience. Occasionally there are some uncomfortable situations with the local police—if you go, make sure you keep all of your paperwork with you at all times—but all the villagers are amazing. The little ten-year-old boys meeting you at the docks at 5 a.m. to load your stuff in the boat, seeing one-acre ponds holding a thousand pintails, and watching a hundred thousand redheads use this huge coastal lagoon is something no hunter can see and not appreciate. I once shot a green-winged, a blue-winged, and a cinnamon teal in three consecutive shots there. I enjoyed watching the bird boys keep tallies of our doves on a hunt, as we could tell they had placed bets on us ahead of time. I've also seen enough decoying redheads to fill a man's bucket for a lifetime, and I feel like I can recollect nearly every volley. On these trips, friendships were formed, cemented, and grown. I can't imagine a life not filled with these experiences.

• • •

Fishing spots also fill my memory bank of favorite places. Small-mouth fishing the New River, trout fishing the mountain streams, bass fishing Lake Ellis at Camp Bryan—I've enjoyed those and so many experiences at tons of other special spots. North Carolina is a blessed state, in that we have a wide array of waters to enjoy year-round. As I said earlier, I grew up trout fishing, and I still have a small group of friends that I do this with every year on a couples trip. It can be as wild as you want on some of the true mountain streams, or you can keep it simple in the stocked streams. Lakes and ponds are all over the state. You can catch bass, crappie, and even some world-class catfish.

I spent many a weekend as a youth going to the "pay to fish" stocked catfish and carp ponds. You would pay $10 to fish, bring your own gear, and then could be awarded some prize money if you caught the biggest fish of the day. We never won, but we would sit out there, occasionally sneak some beer we "found," catch a few, and ultimately end up having to call my parents to get a ride. We told them we were too tired to drive, but I don't think they were ever fooled.

When I was in high school there were many Saturday mornings in April when I would roll out of bed early to meet up with some buddies to fish with my dad at the little trout stream when it had been freshly stocked. If we were lucky, my friends and I would catch a couple, usually after my dad told us exactly where to cast. Meanwhile, his stringer was full at 7:30 a.m. and he was practicing catch and release. I swear, there were days on those streams where it seemed like he could catch a trout in a mud puddle and we couldn't get a bite if we were fishing in the hatchery itself. Still, we would run these little stocked streams all day, only stopping for food and water, and caught more trout in those few years than most will catch in a lifetime.

• • •

I have one good friend whose life cycle has been the opposite of mine. He grew up in eastern NC, and has now moved west. He has learned all the tricks of the trade there, and now owns some property on the Dan River, which has some great smallmouth fishing. We went on the inaugural fishing trip on his new piece of land during my most recent visit there, and I was lucky enough to catch the first smallmouth from this property. That may seem uneventful, but things like this mean a lot to friends and family, and I am sure that both of us will remember that day.

On one of my first-ever weekends as a resident of eastern NC, one of my brother-in-law's friends invited me down to spend the weekend at their house on the South River and participate in what they referred to as the "Rodeo." This was an annual weekend of fishing all day and chasing big drum at night. I jumped at the opportunity, and cut my teeth on the coastal waters of NC that weekend. To this day, I am still great friends with a lot of these guys, and I even got to take my son down to that house on a recent summer fishing trip.

The coastal waters of eastern NC have so much to offer. Offshore fishing is popular, and some of the biggest marlin tournaments on the Atlantic are out of NC. Since I occasionally get seasick, that isn't something I frequent, but I did experience some awesome trips. I saw my best friend from childhood catch a blue marlin on his bachelor trip, and have had some great days catching wahoo and mahi.

But what really gets my attention is the inshore fishing. The coastal rivers here hold drum, speckled trout, flounder, and a host of other fun fish to catch. Catching the big "bull drum" on a fall night is an experience that rivals few others on the water. Sitting in a boat at dusk, listening for the drag to take off, then fighting a 50-pound-plus old giant is so special.

One night, off the reef in Ocracoke, my entire family got to experience an event that I will never forget. With the sun setting over the island, we caught all the state citation-sized bull drum we wanted to. My son was only eight years old at the time, and he reeled in five. He even got a bonus 5-pound speckled trout to top it off. My wife caught some and my then three-year-old daughter even got to help reel some in. The next morning, the guide met us at the tackle shop to officially weigh my son's trout for his citation. It was just a hair over 5 pounds, so it was an official trophy. Watching my son fill out his citation form, and attempt to "sign" his name in cursive on the form, was so innocent and exciting. Those citations are framed in his bedroom today, another commemoration of a special day on the water. We have tried this fishing trip several times since then, but as you likely know, such trips can be hard to duplicate.

I have spent countless days on those coastal waters chasing puppy drum and speckled trout. I have learned some techniques from friends that have been fun and successful, and I have seen parts of these waters that I would never see otherwise. Years ago, our group of friends used to participate in an inshore tournament. The largest combo of trout, drum, and flounder would win. Our house had three teams, and each of them won it once. I will say that I am not much for making hunting or fishing a competition, but winning did feel pretty good. A nice trophy and small cash prize didn't hold a candle to how it felt to spend the day on the water with my friends, though.

Chasing cobia on the beach, fishing the reefs for sheepshead, and surf fishing for pompano are also special challenges on our coastal waters. Fishing from a boat along the shore is great, but I do really enjoy surf fishing. I think this is because my wife and daughter love the beach, and can sit out there all day. As a loving husband and father, my job is to figure out how to get not only my son, but myself as well, to stay out there all day with them. The easiest fix is a surf rod and a bag of bait shrimp. This can keep me occupied for hours, and therefore, the whole family is happy. Really, any time you have a rod in your hands near the water is entertaining. NC has so much to offer, most of which I still haven't even gotten to take a stab at yet. I plan to work on checking some of these items off in the next few years with my kids.

· · ·

In what time I have left, I want to continue growing these memories. I have places that I would love to see that haven't made it across my table yet, and I have other spots that I want to see year in and year out. Never take a spot where you hunt or fish for granted. It may seem like "just a wood duck hole" or "just a little 40-acre piece," but memories can be made there the same as they can on a 10,000-acre hunt club. My favorite places to go aren't a sports arena, or a big city, or a Caribbean beach. They are in small towns, on dirt roads, where you barely have cell service. Nothing fills my heart like a weekend with my family at the hunting cabin, where there is no cell signal. No one is scrolling, no one is watching You-Tube. Your only options are being outside, playing a family game, or simply recalling the day's events. Nothing brings a family or friends closer than good conversation. I think about a time during duck season when I sat at the campfire with my daughter. We were making s'mores and listening to the owls holler at the moon. Innocently, she started sharing stories of her experiences of the day, and they were all so specific to this situation. I was listening as she rambled, and I realized she would never have these experiences at home. Chasing frogs, watching ducks come to roost, and eating at the campfire are exactly why these places are so special.

CHAPTER 5

Outdoor Experiences

Hunting involves so much more than the pursuit of an animal. I once had a guy ask me "So, you just put out decoys and the ducks come to you? Sounds dumb." Boy, do I wish it were that easy sometimes, but that isn't the point. The extra activities during an adventure outdoors are typically the meat of the story.

I have been journaling my hunts for nearly twenty years. For some, a hunt journal includes temperature, wind direction, moon phase, and so on. That is not what I'm interested in. Of course, some of that is included, but for the most part, it is a story of the day. Excerpts include "so and so fell in the swamp while we were shooting mallards," or "so and so had to take an emergency bathroom break standing on a stump in the swamp." Those are the things I recall the most.

I consider myself a man of laughter, and so many funny things happen doing outdoor activities. Some outdoorsmen take their craft too seriously, and miss out on some of the comedy lying on the periphery of most occasions. I have had friends get to the duck blind having left their shells, or even worse their gun, at the truck. The emergency bathroom situations are some of my favorites, as they tend to happen far too often. Nothing puts you in a pickle like bad weather, early mornings, surrounded by woods or water, and needing to go to the bathroom. Hilarity usually ensues.

Murphy's Law is never more in action than when you are in the outdoors. It is hard to have a truly smooth morning without something happening that can throw the day off. If you don't learn to go with it, your day will be ruined. I have learned to prepare, expect something to go wrong, prepare again, and then roll with the punches if it's still not going right. I've seen some dangerous situations unfold, especially when the weather is raw and cold. I've witnessed men fall out of a boat on the river when it was 17 degrees outside. I've spoken to people who have fallen from tree stands, and you routinely hear of misfired weapons that nearly end in a bad situation. The activities outdoors cannot be taken lightly. Safety has to be top priority. Once that is taken care of, everyone can sit back and enjoy the show.

On one occasion, my lifelong best friend was able to join me in my favorite duck blind. The morning was slow, but we did have a drake blue-winged teal sneak in, and he smoked it. In his excitement, he opened the blind door and stepped out as if he were on flat ground. He fell face-first into the swamp, just as my uncle had done years before, and emerged soaking wet. He's always a good sport, and we laughed for days about this. That bluewing sits on a shelf in his living room, another reminder of a great memory.

An outdoorsman never knows what he may see while on a hunt. If you aren't paying attention, something magical may slip right through your fingers. While sea duck hunting in Massachusetts once, I shot my first ever goldeneye. As we waited for the tender boat to come scoop it up, I noticed something in the water. That "something" was a sea lion that quickly popped up and snatched my prize right in front of me. At the time I was upset, but he was just trying to keep himself fed. That experience is worth more than another duck mounted in my living room.

At Reelfoot Lake, during a slow hunting day, I noticed several bald eagles in the sky. Anyone from my age and up gets very excited at the sight of these majestic birds. I went through nearly twenty-five years of life before I saw one. Now they are a little more common, but they are still a magical sight and the most American symbol I can think of. That day, we sat and watched what seemed like hundreds of bald eagles on that lake. They were catching fish, combating in the air, putting on a show. Stuff like this is what makes the outdoors so special. We didn't pull the trigger that day, but all anyone could think of was how cool the eagles were.

I've seen bobcats chasing field mice while I waited for deer to make an appearance, otters catching bass on a duck pond, and a fox trying to snatch my turkey decoy on a hunt. Sometimes, you see something so unbelievable that you are afraid folks won't believe you, but they don't have to. If you saw it, enjoy that memory, whether or not you were lucky enough to have a friend who was there and can vouch for you.

• • •

One of my favorite stories from a fishing trip has nothing to do with any fish that were caught. Earlier in this book I mentioned the buddies that I go smallmouth fishing with from time to time. We are all great friends who have known one another since high school, and we always enjoy any time we get to spend together. On one of our trips to the New River, my uncle wanted to tag along. He's always a source of great tales and hilarious antics, so no one was going to argue with him coming along. He had set us up with a camping spot, and even had our tents ready for us to use when we arrived.

The first morning, we decided to take our kayaks up to the dam in Fries, Virginia. This is a great fishing spot, and it would also allow us to float downriver and fish for six miles on the way back to our campsite. We all got our boats in and started the short trip upstream to get to the falls of the dam. In my opinion, this is one of the most beautiful spots on the New River. The water is deeper here than anywhere else on the river, and on this day, it was as clear as the beaches in the Caribbean. From every depth, fish could be seen swimming among the giant boulders that are scattered throughout the water here. The backdrop of picturesque cascading water adds the perfect touch to this amazing place.

The five of us spent about an hour fishing this spot. We paddled around the rocks, fishing under the waterfall and everywhere else in the area. While we were fishing, a stranger paddled up and joined us. He seemed to be about our age, and offered us the typical head nod as he approached. We never spoke with him, as the sound of the falling water made it impossible to hear, but he seemed to be a nice enough guy. Soon after he arrived, my friend Chase paddled up to me and suggested that we go ahead and head down the river. We signaled for the rest of the guys to follow suit, and everyone but my uncle saw the signal. He was on the far side of the river, talking to the stranger who had arrived, and we even saw him pull his phone out to take a picture. We thought nothing of it, as he is always a social butterfly and seems to make friends everywhere he goes. Unable to reach him, the four of us decided to head on, as my uncle knows these waters like the back of his hand and would have no problem catching up later.

The next three hours were great. We ended up tying our boats together and floating the river like an armada. We caught a few more fish, but we mostly just talked and spent time catching up. This was a much-needed time for us, as days spent together nowadays are hard to come by. The weather was perfect, the water was clear, and the fellowship was awesome.

Just as we approached the bridge by our campsite, I looked over my shoulder to see my uncle paddling downstream in his typical, full-speed approach. He was so locked into his mission that he didn't even notice us floating along the bank. I yelled for him, and when he looked over, he did a double take. The look of confusion was obvious from 50 yards away. He got closer, took off his sunglasses and exclaimed, "Chase!? How the hell did you get here?"

As you can imagine, we were all just as confused as he was. We all chimed in, "What are you talking about?" My uncle got even closer and said, "I have been fishing with you all morning at the dam, and I left before you did. How did you get here so fast?" That's when we put it together. Unaware that a stranger had arrived, and being that the man had similar features and clothes, my uncle just assumed he had been fishing with Chase. After we returned to camp, we got the full story. My uncle spent three hours hanging out with a total stranger, but treating him like he had known him for years. They ate together, took pictures of one another, and caught several fish. At one point, they even got out of their boats and climbed the wall of the dam to fish for a while. There is no telling what kind of stories he shared with this guy, but for some reason, the stranger was too nice to ever question my uncle.

To this day, we laugh about this story every time we talk about fishing. What a random memory my uncle created by simply being friendly. At the same time, though, I often think about what kind of stories the stranger is telling about this situation. An older gentleman approached him on his solo fishing trip, spent the entire day side by side with him, and talked his ear off all the while. What I would give to be able to find this guy and hear his side of the story.

Sometimes, the humor we enjoy in the outdoors originates not from the people we're with, but from the birds and animals as they go about their daily lives. On a spring morning several years ago, a good friend and I decided to head to a small lease I had just outside of town. I knew there were some turkeys there, but my familiarity with the land was not good. The other lease members and I had built a nice wooden bridge to cross the creek, just where you head out of the main, front field and head into the woods. Not knowing any better, I decided that this would be a great place to park the truck. In hindsight, tall timber along a creek does sound like the perfect place for a turkey to roost, and a terrible place to park the truck. We stood by the truck as we put on our boots. As the morning crept on, we started listening carefully for the sound of an early-morning gobbler. To my surprise, what I heard instead was a loud thud on my windshield at first light; then, the sound of wings flying away from us. I had somehow managed to park directly beneath a gobbler, which had been watching us all morning. The thud I heard was a pile of poop he unceremoniously dropped on my windshield before he left us. The hunt that morning was fun, but that memory is one of the funniest.

• • •

Some of the spectacles that can be experienced in nature are so awe-inspiring that it makes you sit back and gasp at how abundant and amazing our wildlife can be. I've sat in the hardwood bottom of a gameland and heard what had to be dozens of turkeys gobbling all around me. I have seen flocks of thousands of redheads and bluebills on the sound, flying together in what appears to be a black cloud in the sky. I've seen schools of speckled trout feeding on glass minnow pods that appeared to be miles long. It seems unbelievable now that America's wildlife was pushed to near extinction within the past century. Seeing the efforts of conservation pay off is something to be admired and respected.

Sometimes the events we see on our hunting or fishing trips are things that are unlikely to happen more than once in a lifetime. A good example comes from a long-ago deer hunt with my dad. We were sitting in the tree stand where I have seen some of the most fantastic things happen in the deer woods. It's on an old log bed on a hardwood ridge in the foothills, in the same piece of forest mentioned earlier when I shot the turkey on my parents' family farm. My dad had been having some health issues, and he really didn't feel like going, but I had a strange feeling and pressured him into going. Although he was exhausted and a bit irritable, I felt that an evening sit out in the woods was exactly what he needed. Hesitantly, he agreed, and we made the long trek to the old reliable ladder stand.

We had does bleating all around us and running everywhere, even as my dad put no emphasis on scent control, as he was smoking a cigarette in the stand; or on sound control, as we were laughing uncontrollably a few times about silly stuff from the day. You could tell that there was something special about what was going on. Here you have two men, honestly not even really trying to be stealthy, and all around us we had deer action. We watched countless does work up and down the ridge, occasionally stopping to eat some acorns. They were all far more vocal than I had ever heard, which I definitely noticed to be unique.

Out of the corner of my eye, I spotted a large deer running into view. When I pulled up my binoculars, I saw a nice buck in full sprint, his tongue hanging from his mouth as he tried to catch his breath. I could tell he was a nice eight-pointer, but my dad was unaware because his vision just doesn't allow him to see the fine details of a deer while he is in the woods. The buck chased a doe all over the ridge where we sat until he was flat out of breath, then proceeded to mount and breed her right in front of us at 40 yards. When the buck had finished his task, my dad pulled up his muzzleloader and dropped him right in his tracks. I have never seen this happen since, and that is something my dad and I still talk about every time we see that head mount on his living room wall.

• • •

An often overlooked piece of the hunting experience doesn't really have anything to do with what is going on outside. These events are frequently cathartic and benefit a man's brain and psyche. Life is stressful, money can be tight, family can be sick, a host of other issues may be on his mind—but in the brief moment that a big buck walks out, or a turkey is gobbling just around the corner, nothing else matters. You can ask me what my bank account looks like while a drake wigeon is circling and whistling, and I won't be able to mumble a sentence. In those moments, we are truly care-free. The beauty doesn't only stop there; it carries over to those who are with us.

I think back to a good friend who for quite a while was deal-ing with a pretty harsh divorce situation. I could hear in his voice over the phone that his life felt like it was falling apart. He needed a getaway with friends, and the trip we took together to duck hunt in Ocracoke turned out to be exactly what he needed.

The first day, he hunted with my uncle, who is one of his best friends. The hunting was not good, borderline terrible to most, but we weren't in any position to complain. We were all together, doing what we loved and enjoying each other's company.

On multiple occasions, my friend would have to step out of the blind and walk away, as he was having in-depth conversa-tions about his divorce with his attorney. We would try to make light of the situation when he returned, but the look in his eyes made it obvious that he was not in a healthy mental space. It was a strange situation. I wanted to help, but I had no idea what to do.

Sometimes you just have to be there for someone, but for a man, it is always a challenge when you can't solve a problem.

On the last afternoon of the trip, most of our party had nearly given up on the hunt. With warm weather, no wind, and an unseasonably low tide, hunting on the reef had been abysmal. My uncle and our friend and I had been in a stake blind all morning, cooking breakfast and talking, with no birds to be seen. As the rest of the group started heading in, we decided we weren't ready to give up just yet.

You see, my uncle and I suffer from a mental delusion that my friends refer to as "Odell Optimism." No matter the situation, no matter the evidence presented, and no matter the circumstance, we always seem to convince ourselves that something great is about to happen. We are the kings of the "one more cast" or "30 more minutes" state of mind when the rest of the guys are ready to hang it up. We put the Odell Optimism to the test on this day, as we decided we wanted to spend our last remaining evening on the reef in the curtain blind. Since those blinds are only big enough for two hunters, our friend decided he would just go to the stake blind about 200 yards down the reef and sit by himself. We wanted to be there for him, but he insisted.

When we hopped in the blind, the decoys were all high and dry, as the low tide was in full effect. It was sunny and over 70 degrees, with absolutely zero wind. This is what anyone with any sense at all would call absolutely terrible conditions. Still, we had our guns loaded and our eyes to the sky.

The next two hours were filled with stories from the trip and years past. We laughed until we cried, and almost completely forgot about what we were even doing. In reality, the duck conditions were bad, but the weather for sitting outside near the water and hanging out was perfect. I have never laughed so much as I did that afternoon, until the unexpected happened.

In the middle of one of my uncle's stories, I heard the distinct chirpy whistle of a drake pintail. I grabbed my uncle's arm to get him to stop talking, as he never heard it. Years of Grateful Dead concerts and the blasts of thousands of shotgun shells has left him with little to no ability to hear. He knew what I meant when I grabbed him though, and we both tightened up. As I looked over my right shoulder, there they were. Twelve beautiful drake pintails, all circling in perfectly to come socialize with their decoy friends. Before we had time to say another word, it was time to shoot.

Shooting out of a curtain blind is not rookie-level stuff in the waterfowling world. As you sit, your head is level with the water line, and with no backdrop, it can be difficult to judge depths. Luckily, we had both done this for years, and these birds were about to land on our heads. We hopped up and shot our birds. Just like that, a trip of disappointment was totally redeemed. We called the guide to pick us up, as sunset was rapidly approaching. On the way he grabbed our friend, who had been sitting by himself for hours.

When the boat pulled up, we could see our friend smiling, looking completely different from the way he had looked over the previous forty-eight hours. When the boat stopped, he jumped out and ran to meet us, exclaiming "I saw those pintails!! How cool was that!!" We couldn't help but agree, but mostly we were just shocked at how happy he seemed. As it turns out, the lack of wind allowed the sound to carry across the water extremely well. As he lay on the bench in the blind, just enjoying the sunny afternoon, he listened to us talk and laugh while the hours passed. Then to top it all off, he just so happened to have stepped onto the deck of the blind to relieve himself when the pintails were coming in, so he saw the whole shot.

That short period of time for him to sit and reflect in God's glorious outdoors and listen to friends share stories was all the therapy he needed at that moment in his life. Watching the ducks work and watching us make the shots put him right over the top. We were all put into that situation through the power of Odell Optimism, and in this situation, it worked in more ways than one.

Sharing these times in the outdoors not only helps us help ourselves, but also builds friendships. I mentioned this earlier, but it cannot be overstated. A day in the duck blind, or a day on a road trip, or a night at deer camp cleaning a buck offers nothing but time to grow a friendship. This creates a bond that cannot be broken; you have experienced something so special that can never be taken away.

Our closest personal relationships also are often made stronger through times we enjoy together in the outdoors. A great example of this occurred when my immediate family and I spent the weekend after Thanksgiving 2024 at our hunting club chasing some deer. I decided to wake the family up one morning and drag them into the duck blind, knowing from my scouting efforts and the weather conditions that it was going to be a slow day. Honestly, I just thought it would be more entertaining for me, so I made a selfish call.

About thirty minutes into the hunt, we noticed deer all over the trail cameras, and my son was getting frustrated that he was missing out. He was a preteen who loved the outdoors, but needed some action. Finally, my wife decided that she would go with him to the deer stand, something she rarely, if ever, does. My daughter stayed with me. We got to watch a few late-morning mallards work and to blow a duck call and eat some snacks.

When my daughter and I wrapped up, we headed back to the cabin and saw two drake buffleheads on the pond. She got very excited, noticing how brilliant they looked in the sunlight. Never in the history of this property have we ever seen a bufflehead on this pond, so the sight alone was a treat. She asked if she could try to shoot one, and I gladly obliged. We snuck around and got into position. On her first-ever shot with a shotgun, she water-swatted a bufflehead. She was excited, and still to this day recalls that event every time we discuss duck hunting. It was a shared experience that she will think about every time she sees that little butter ball mounted on her wall.

Meanwhile, my wife and son were having a blast in the deer stand. They saw tons of deer, and even a few small bucks. My wife loved it, and talked it about over lunch at the local greasy spoon. That evening, when making our plans to hunt, my wife asked if she could sit with my son. I acted disappointed, but was actually excited. They needed this time together. Naturally, the relationship between parents and preteens can be a little bit intense at times. There is not a lot of time to enjoy each other's company; it's more of a mad rush to get to places and instruct how to do things. This evening, while they sat in the blind, they played UNO, discussed life in more detail than they had in years, and laughed and smiled. I heard a shot from their blind, so I knew a deer was down, but I couldn't contact them on the phone as they were in the swamp bottom with no service. I was planning to head that way and help them with the process, when to my surprise, they came pulling up, loudly playing their music and laughing together, with a big doe in the back of the ATV. This was an experience they shared, and it grew that bond tremendously. This weekend could easily be overlooked as just another one of our family trips to the club, but I am telling you, these are the special times a family needs to grow stronger.

Bonds can be grown through multiple generations while hunting as well. My son has been fortunate enough to get to spend many days in the woods with his grandfathers, enjoying fishing, deer hunting, and even turkey hunting. I am always excited when he gets these opportunities, but I really learned their significance over one weekend trip with my father.

Every year, we do our best to get my son and my father together to hunt as often as we can. During this particular trip, it was clear that my son was starting to come into his own as a deer hunter. He no longer talked loudly in the stand, he could spot a deer through the woods, and he had become quite the shot with his rifle. We were at my parents' house, and he and my dad made a decision to hunt every chance they could that weekend. I immediately obliged this opportunity, as this meant I could hang around the house with my mother and spend some quality time with her. Deer hunting is something I have grown more fond of over the past few years, just by sharing my son's passion, but I was by no means desperate to spend the entire weekend in the deer stand.

The two of them spent every waking moment of Friday and Saturday chasing whitetails. It happened to be one of those times during the season when everything was in a lull. Not even the best hunting spots on the farm saw much action, if any. The woods were quiet, and the deer seemed to be nocturnal. After Saturday evening's hunt, they both were bummed. We ate dinner and my son fell asleep on the couch, exhausted from his adventures. I went to bed early that night, and planned to get up first thing and pack up the truck to head home. When I got out of bed, though, I found that both my dad and my son were nowhere to be found. They were back in the woods again.

I packed up the truck and hopped in the shower. As soon as I got dressed, my phone rang. It was my dad, so I quickly answered, hoping for good news. When I answered, my dad said, "Didn't see anything, we are headed back." I felt dejected. I wanted this to be special for them, and it had turned out to be a total bust. Then, I heard a little giggle in the background from my son. My dad said, "Yeah, no deer around here. I guess we just don't know what we are doing." Then my son busted out laughing loudly. I knew what they were up to—this was a planned prank. Quickly, I said "I'm on my way!" and hung up the phone.

I drove my truck as close as I could to their stand, and when I walked close enough to see them, they were still sitting in the ladder stand, talking and laughing. When they saw me, they got down and started heading my way. Sure enough, not 20 yards from where I stood, was a little six-point buck. This was no record-setting deer, but it was even more special than that. This was their deer. They put in the hours, sitting together patiently. My son grabbed the horns and just smiled at my dad. We took tons of pictures, and then we loaded it up in the truck. As I got in my truck, my son said he wanted to ride home with Papa on the four-wheeler. Of course he did.

For a moment, a little touch of jealousy ran through my veins. For all of my life, I experienced the special moments with my dad. And for all of my son's life, I shared the special moments with him. Now, here they were, getting their own special moment. When they passed me on the four-wheeler, flying down the path and laughing, those feelings quickly subsided. For the rest of both of their lives, this will be their experience. I was overwhelmed with emotion as I watched them drive off, and I had to fight back tears at how truly special this was.

• • •

The quality time spent at hunting camp with friends and family is something that cannot be reproduced elsewhere. If you are lucky enough to get to spend a weekend at hunting or fishing camp, you know those forty-eight to seventy-two hours are going to be an all-around treat. Obviously, your main intent is to chase game, so that will be a highlight of most of the time you spend there. With that said, there are only so many hours of daylight, so there are always some extracurricular activities waiting for you. Often, at a cabin in the woods or on the water, your options are limitless. The world is your playground if you know what to look for.

Countless nights at the old hunting club in Pamlico County were spent night fishing. We would drive the ATV down to a dead-end road, where an old dock was built out onto the water. There were no dock lights, so what little light we got from our phones had to lead the way. You had to watch for missing boards, sometimes having to deal with a gap three boards wide. Once you made it to the shelter, though, you were fishing. We would bring speakers and a cooler, and sit out there til the wee hours of the morning. Our rods were always in the water, but I can only recall a handful of fish actually being reeled in. That was never the point, though. We were there just because we could be, and that's the beauty of it.

Hunting season usually coincides with several sports seasons, especially in the fall and winter. On a Saturday evening after a hunt, there is always a football game to watch while sitting around the camp, sharing stories. With sports on in the background, naturally, some good-natured junk talking will almost always break out. It will start when rival teams are playing one another. Maybe you have a UNC football fan in camp on the day when their team is playing NC State. The nature of the beast is hard to control, so words will always be said to try to get under the other person's skin. Once the talk is started, especially with my group of friends, some form of competition will almost always develop. I have two great friends who are wonderful people and world-class junk talkers. When together, they are constantly ribbing and poking at one another, trying to start some sort of competition. It sometimes may be a game of pool, or it may be who can catch the most fish, but on one occasion, it was a foot race.

Keep in mind, we were all approaching forty at the time. In fact, one of the guys was well past that ripe old age. He had played college football, and was never scared of a challenge. My other friend began to "poke the bear." He was closer to my age, and was honestly a pretty sneaky athlete. I knew he wasn't scared of a competition either, so the rest of us at camp began to push for this race to take place. Finally, they agreed to settle it in the backyard in Pamlico County at just past midnight.

I volunteered to be the finish-line judge, so I marked off what I estimated to be about 30 yards. My football player friend laced his shoes up tight, while my other friend removed his altogether. Barefoot vs. sneakers, both too old to be sprinting, but we were about to see it go down. As the official starter I had them take their marks. After multiple false starts, on what may have been the fifth attempt, we had a real race. I expected my friend who had played football to leave the other in the dirt, and honestly I think everyone else did, too. To my surprise, my barefoot friend got off the start line like Usain Bolt. His start was so strong that in the short 30-yard race, the football player couldn't make up the ground.

To this day, watching two middle-aged men sprint in the dark is one of the funniest things I have ever witnessed. Fortunately for me, though, they weren't finished. The wisecracks continued. Accusations of cheating were flying around, and the only solution was for a second race, double or nothing. Their marks were quickly taken this time, and the looks on their faces were far more serious. The starter yelled "GO." Immediately, not even one full step into the race, my barefoot friend fell flat on his face as if someone had jerked his feet out from under him. He went into a full scorpion position, chin on the ground, and the heels of his bare feet coming all the way up from behind to kick him in the back of the head. No one spoke for fifteen minutes. The laughter was so loud I am surprised the neighbors didn't call the cops.

We may never know who the winner of that race truly was, and we will likely never get a rematch. To me, I know who the real winner was, but I'll never tell either of them. That kind of moment is what you come to expect on a weekend at camp. Expect the unexpected, and have as much fun as you can while you are there. Your free time at camp is a blessing, to be honored and cherished. Don't waste time arguing over where to hunt the next day, or what deer you should shoot. Those conversations can take place on group text threads during the week.

• • •

It is easy to get caught up in the competition of hunting. Everyone wants to have a picture to post of the most ducks, the biggest buck, the most fish, and so on. If that's what you're focused on, you are going to spend a lot of time disappointed and frustrated. Most young hunters spend too much time in that mind frame, and many of them never outgrow it. We are given an opportunity as outdoorsmen to spend time in some amazing places and experience some of God's greatest wonders. If we don't enjoy it while we can, we'll all too soon find out that our opportunities have passed, and from what I gather speaking to the older generation, the time comes for your body to stop hunting far before your mind is ready to do so.

CHAPTER 6

Food, Fellowship, and Music

I am so engaged and obsessed with my hobby that I have dabbled in every aspect, even spending a year attempting to master taxidermy. I mounted several ducks for my friends and family, working in my garage and calling a taxidermist friend weekly for advice. I mounted about ten birds, all of which are still on display somewhere, but none of which I would consider to be remotely good. Eventually, I fell out of love with this hobby, and I moved on to making my own decoys, prompted by one of life's milestone events.

The year my son was born, my duck season was cut short. His birthdate is January 4, right in the middle of the best part of the season. I may sound a little salty about this, because believe it or not, at the time I was. I have now realized how perfect it is to celebrate a birthday during duck season, but at the time, I was depressed. As new parents, we didn't know if we were coming or going, so we needed all hands on deck. For the rest of the season, I was at home, helping however I could to take care of my new child.

The season before, I had begun to dabble is some sea duck hunting with my brother-in-law and one of his friends. My best idea to pass the time during my baby-duty-at-home lockdown was to make my own decoys. Sea ducks tend to be very easy to decoy, and some old-timers use something as simple as a two-liter bottle painted black. I felt like I could definitely make something better than that. I did some research, got the supplies, and during the next two months spent all of my free time in the garage, grinding. I made four dozen scoters, a mixture of surfs and commons. I ordered the heads pre-carved, so I only had to paint them. The rest of the presentation was all made by yours truly. I carved the bodies out of foam, wrapped them in burlap and tile mastic, added railroad spikes as a keel, and painted them all. To my surprise, they looked great. The following season, my brother-in-law and I hunted over them, and even killed a few surf scoters over them. It was quite the feeling of satisfaction to see them floating out in the Pungo River, staying afloat and drawing in birds. As time passed, though, the available time for me to get to the river and chase those birds dwindled, so I ended up selling the decoys to a true sea duck hunter who resided at the coast. I hope he is still shooting over them today.

As satisfying as that whole experience was, the desire to continue making decoys was gone. It took me years to realize why taxidermy and decoy making just weren't my thing, even though they brought me some pleasure. I didn't enjoy it because I was alone. Just me, in the garage, no fellowship, no camaraderie, not even any laughs. As much as I am glad that I was able to give these hobbies a try, I now know that the fellowship is what I am after. Even today, whenever I visit my friend's house at Camp Bryan, I see one of my decoys on the shelf there, displayed with several other prized decoys my friend has collected. It serves a much better purpose there. Now, I can tell the story about it with friends, and I know I'll never be in that garage working on decoys by myself again.

· · ·

There is one aspect of my life that holds nearly as much favor in my brain as hunting, and that is music. I am a huge music fan, always have been. My father played in a rock band, and that's even how my parents met. My dad was the drummer and my mom's brother was the singer; thus, my amazing parents met in the most fitting way ever. I grew up on classic rock of the 1960s, '70s, and '80s. I remember the local classic rock station running their "two-fer Tuesday" playlist. It would be back-to-back songs by the same group, and my father made a game of giving me three chances to name which band it was. Usually, I could figure it out by the second song.

My brother was seven years older, so when I was in middle school and stretching my wings in all things cool, he brought to me all sorts of new '90s music that got me hooked even more. Throughout high school, my friends were all music fans. I spent much of my youth playing the drums, and I still try to do so when I get the chance. I spent weekends going to concerts, and there was always something loud blasting from the speakers of my 1987 GMC Jimmy, with its fancy twelve-disc changer in the back. This obsession never stopped, and now my entire family feels the same way. Music is a part of our lives that is always present. You will never catch us at the hunting club or on the boat without a wireless speaker and music blaring.

For some strange reason, my brain compartmentalizes events and will often associate certain locations and events with a specific band or song. To this day, a song may be my favorite to listen to at the moment, and gets put on repeat for a weekend trip, and from then on, that is the soundtrack of the event in my mind. Every time I hear that song later, I think of that time and place. When "Older Women" by Ronnie McDowell comes across my music station, I am immediately taken back to the weekend about twelve years ago at our little club in Northampton County with two of my great friends.

I had put together a hunt party for the gameland that surrounded our property in Northampton. My lifelong friend was living in the Outer Banks at the time. His hunting opportunities had been limited due to his busy work schedule, but he took some time off to make this happen. I also invited another friend I had recently started hunting with. He had married one of my wife's sorority sisters, and we quickly became friends once we met. The two of my friends had never met, but I knew them both well enough to be sure they would hit it off.

As soon as we arrived to the cabin on Thursday night, we grilled a big meal and started catching up. Just as I suspected, my hunting buddies soon became fast friends. In fact, they still stay in touch and hunt together to this day. That weekend was full of adventures. At one point, I had to rescue one of my friends while he was napping. A large black snake was slithering right at him, and would have undoubtedly scared him to death had it woken him up. We spent hours chasing gobblers all over the property and had more action than we expected. There were multiple close calls, several working birds, and I even managed to kill one midday with my buddies hiding in the background handling the calls.

The nights were filled with music and food. We all took turns playing songs, and at some point one of my friends pulled up the classic "Older Women." The other friend showed off his baritone voice and serenaded us while we laughed. For some reason, that song is what I think of every time I think of that weekend. The three of us reunited in Mexico a few years ago on a duck hunting trip, and on the truck ride home from an afternoon quail shoot, I hooked up to our driver's radio and played the tune. The Mexican driver had obviously never heard it, but I bet he can still remember the three of us singing it at the top of our lungs riding down the back roads of Carboneras, Mexico.

• • •

There have been countless nights listening to all grades of music at Camp Bryan while we sat out under the stars and thought about our day. Camp Bryan is a hunt club unlike any other I have been to. There are over thirty members, and most of them have houses, all on a row along the lakeshore. Folks drive around, going from place to place, stopping in to speak when they can.

The camp is nearly 11,000 acres, all contiguous behind a locked gate. Once you are in there, it feels like you are in an Old West gold rush town a hundred years ago, other than the occasional shoot-out. All people think about is the game they are hunting and the food they are cooking. The lake is plentiful with bass and gators, so you can always enjoy that in the spring if your morning turkey hunt isn't successful. You can also ease around the property to a viewing spot, where you can watch what we have always referred to as the "peep show," where you watch ducks coming in and leaving the impoundment at dusk. All these activities, though, have a soundtrack in my head. In the ATV, we are always listening to music, and late at night while we are cooking, we are listening to music, sometimes even a little too late into the night.

A great story always comes to mind. It happened just before my daughter was born, and the music and celebration nearly got the best of me. I was down there with two friends and one of the friend's dad, who is a member. One of those buddies tends to bring out the best in me, in the worst kind of way. We hadn't seen each other in a while, and we were so excited to listen to the new Tyler Childers album that night. Before we knew it, it was way too late, and we had to go to bed. My friend's dad and I were hunting together the next morning, and I knew he was going to be ready to rock-and-roll early.

I fell asleep on the couch, fully dressed in my hunting clothes from the previous day. I even still had my face mask around my neck. In my confusion after my early wake-up, I grabbed my gear, hopped in the truck, and we took off. I was far from chipper that morning; instead, I would consider myself to have been suffering from a severe lack of rest. We parked what seemed like 5 miles away from the plot we were hunting, and began the walk in what I can only recall as the darkest morning in history. When we finally arrived, we set up on the edge of the woods, and it was barely 5 a.m. We had over an hour before anything was going to happen.

Now, in hindsight, this was genius. I was napping in the woods, lying on the ground like a dead starfish, when the sound of wings flapping shook me awake. Sure enough, hens were roosted in the trees we had just walked under. Had we come in any later, we would have spooked them and the morning would have been a wash.

In the distance, to my left, I heard a gobble that sounded close enough to get excited about. I sat up in my gobbler lounger, with the low-hanging limbs of the bay bushes and hardwoods in front of us. We were so hidden it wasn't even fair, and I needed all the odds in my favor. As the sun began to poke out, we saw two gobblers easing out of the back corner, about 75 yards out. They immediately went into full strut when they saw all the hens in the plot, and luckily just cruised straight down the center of the field right in front of us. When they presented a shot, we counted down—3, 2, 1, and BOOM!—double on gobblers accomplished before the sun even had a chance to get rid of the dew on the clover. Not many places where you can get friend time like that the night before, then a successful turkey hunt the next day.

I also recall many nights logging on to some bootleg music-streaming system at the old hunt club in Pamlico, listening to Widespread Panic live at Red Rocks, sitting in my buddy's truck. We would hop in the truck after dinner, roll the windows down, and jam out. Since the Red Rocks amphitheater is across the country, the music started much later than normal Eastern time. It would be late, just starting to cool off from the hot summer day, but still too hot to leave the windows up. The weekend we were down there annually seemed to always coincide with the Red Rocks concert, as it is the same weekend in June every year. Without fail, every time we did this, we would stay up far too late, jamming and celebrating our favorite songs, and ultimately leave the windows down. Mosquitoes would fill the cab, and often a solid sheet of morning dew would be thick on the truck seats. We never cared, and in particular I didn't, as it was never my truck, but it is a very vivid musical memory.

Almost all my favorite songs trigger a memory connected to a special place. This is another way that God keeps my mind on what is important. I love music so much that I listen to it loud and proud every day. And every day, I am reminded of a time and place with good friends doing what I love.

• • •

Food is another factor that finds its way into every fun occasion. An oyster roast at the duck camp, a fresh, grilled backstrap on a Saturday night, or even a local restaurant you frequent at a certain location are all forms of continuing your connection with friends and amplifying the event you just participated in.

After a long day of fishing, a good Low Country boil is a great way to get all the guys around a table, sharing stories and making memories. I vividly recall a hot August afternoon after a day of fishing on the Pamlico. We had caught some blue crabs that day, and bought a pile of other goodies for a Low Country boil. We cooked, we laughed, we sang, and most importantly, we shared time together. After I dumped that pot full of food out on the table just outside the garage, the boys started loading up their plates. A day of fishing will get you as hungry as a teenager. Just as the food was starting to cool off enough to eat, we spotted a nasty coastal thunderstorm brewing in the distance. Before we could get a bite, a brutal downpour rolled in. I'll never forget that while the rest of us hid in the garage from the lightning and rain, trying to eat our food, one of my good friends sat out in the middle of the yard, right by the burner where we had been cooking. The storm wasn't bothering him in the least, and he was ripping into blue crabs so fast his fingers were bleeding. We tried to coax him inside, but he said "I'm already wet now, just let me eat in peace!" Now, that's what I mean when I say hungry as a teenager.

• • •

Neupamba Duck Club, which I have had the pleasure to visit on several occasions, really gets the true meaning of a hunting camp meal. When you arrive the night before your hunt, there will always be a member or two in the huge industrial kitchen slaving away. You can be surprised with anything from prime rib to spaghetti, but you can bet the house that it will be delicious. I have been able to help make a few meals here, and it's always great to hear comments from the members and guests. Obviously, most folks are hungry enough that anything tastes good to them, but they have also been around the block a few times, so they know good food when they see it.

Once the meal is prepared, the bell rings announcing it's time for everyone to come to the kitchen. The members and guests gather, say a blessing, and then the guests are asked to make their plates first. In my opinion, this special tradition is perfect, and exactly what I love to be a part of. The member I attend with is very thoughtful in his meals. Last time, we steamed carrots, made London broil, and our other friend capped it off with some crème brûlée. Now, that is a duck camp meal for the ages. Everyone went back for seconds.

The real kicker, though, is breakfast the next day. You wake up early, drink some coffee, and draw for blinds. There is usually an unbelievable amount of junk talking and plotting at this meeting. Everyone is still crusty eyed, but they spent all night thinking about wind, temperature, sun placement, and where they think they will be the most successful. As you draw your blinds, everyone begins the mad dash for the locker area to get dressed and loaded up. On a cold, wintry day, the boat ride from the house to the impoundments can be downright snotty. It's dark and cold, but the anticipation eases those struggles away with no problem. Once you arrive at the dike, you load up the ATV, head to your blind, then trudge to your spot to set up.

I have never experienced a hunt here that wasn't epic. At first light, loads and loads of pintails and wigeon come pouring in from off the river. The sounds they make get everyone, even the dog, excited. Wigeon and pintails whistling, teal peeping, gadwalls beeping, and even the occasional black duck or mallard calling. The entire landscape is open, other than the occasional island bushes, so you can see the ducks from every direction.

If you were wise enough, or lucky enough to pick a blind with a good wind at your back, you can stand in the pit and watch, totally unseen, as flocks of wigeon and pintails soar out of the stratosphere, locked up all the way into your decoy spread. It induces a noise out of me that no other situation does. I will often audibly grunt when I see a duck decoying in perfectly, and I tend to grunt a lot in this place. Naturally, this lush and amazing environment often results in limits of ducks. It may take you thirty minutes, or it may take you down to the deadline, which is the time decided on by members when hunting is to stop. Setting a deadline allows the ducks to come in unbothered and get comfortable; that way you will have a chance to limit out again on another day. Once you wrap up, the decoys are picked up, pictures are taken, and all the gear is hauled back to the house and unloaded. Then, the guys all work together to clean ducks under the shelter. If you aren't helping there, your job is in the kitchen, whipping up whatever breakfast you think will be appreciated by the group. As you can imagine, after a morning of all this activity, a man can build up quite a ravenous hunger. Once breakfast is cooked, the same tradition ensues. Bell rings, folks come, blessing is said, then the guests and members make plates, sit at the big table in the dining room, and talk. Stories of missed opportunities and great shots, stories of mishaps and amazing sights. As a natural talker, I have to hold myself back from sharing sometimes, even though I want everyone around to know all the incredible stuff I saw; it truly is that special to me. But it's just as good to listen, because everyone there experienced something just as unique, and I love to hear it. That is how you make something memorable out of a meal, in my opinion.

• • •

Nothing puts people shoulder-to-shoulder longer than a table full of steamed oysters. Oyster roasts, at the hunting club or not, are some of my favorite gatherings. About twenty years ago, one of my best friends and I were invited to Hyde County to hunt a friend's impoundment. We had the entire place to ourselves, and had one of those hunts that solidifies why you get up and go. We dealt with nearly exclusively green-winged teal for the day, but it was a non-stop attack. We shot terribly, missed more than I care to admit, but we did kill our limit.

After the ride home that evening, my friend and I decided that the only way to really celebrate was with some oysters. We bought a bushel, started steaming, and he and I, along with another friend we called in for help, polished off the whole bag. I can think of countless times when a bag of oysters was our plan for a meal, and nothing else.

On a lucky weekend long, long ago, my uncle and my best friend were both drawn for blinds at Lake Mattamuskeet on the same day. The lake's draw system allows sixteen people to be drawn for a two-day period, every Tuesday-Wednesday and every Friday-Saturday. There are sixteen blinds, so you're assigned a blind for each day. The bonus kicker is that each person drawn can bring two guests. This meant that our crowd had six folks hunting together for the weekend, so we went ahead and booked a trailer at one of the rental camps by Harris's Steak House. Instead of simply walking to the steak house for dinner, we went to a local seafood dealer, and bought a bushel of the dirtiest oysters you've ever seen, but we got them for a steal. We washed and steamed and worked our butts off getting them clean enough to eat. Then, as the last load was dumped out of the bag to go in the steamer, a dead rat rolled out of the bag with them. To say we were disgusted is an understatement, but don't think we didn't finish eating them all. It takes a lot to gross out a duck hunter enough to not finish his meal.

• • •

A breakfast at a small-time diner is a great way to warm your bones and your soul after a cold duck hunt. There is a local establishment called Claudine's, very close to our camp in Northampton. My children think of it as five-star dining, mainly because whenever we go there, everyone is starving. Their options are seemingly limitless, the food is fantastic, and the ladies working are so welcoming that it just adds an exclamation point to any day in the woods, good or bad. There are many places like that all over small towns throughout rural North Carolina. A breakfast at Wayside in Aurora used to be a real treat, with pancakes the size of your plate, or getting a pizza burger at the Da Nite grill in Bethel. These staples keep young hunters nourished through a long day, which is good because it takes a miracle for hunters to take time out to cook for themselves while chasing game.

A special treat I often offer to the kids hunting with me is a bacon-fried honey bun. My son, nephews, and all other young guns that frequent the blind with me have grown to think of this as one of their favorite parts of a special hunt. I cook a pound of bacon in my old, trusty cast-iron skillet, and then let the honey buns sit in the grease for about ten seconds per side—just enough to soak up some bacon flavor and crisp up the sugar. It may sound questionable, but just ask the boys. This has become as much of a staple on a family hunt as any other line item.

This fellowship around food and music is what I truly treasure. Sitting around a fire, listening to music, sharing stories of the day while eating whatever you decide to throw on the grill, is the best way a man can end a day. Stories are told here, connections are made, and some stories even happen while you are sitting there. I have had total strangers become lifelong friends after a night shucking oysters and sharing tales of the day and days past.

My son can tend to be a bit quiet, seemingly shy to some. I have no idea where he got that from, but I think he is mostly observing a lot of the time, whereas I tend to take the lead in a conversation. I bring him to these situations as often as possible, and he gets more out of it than I typically understand in the moment. He listens to the stories, and I know this because he will bring them up later in another setting; he remembers the people, and I know this because he recalls them when we see them again. I know he eats the food, because that's probably his favorite part of all the events. He also listens to the music, which I know because I'll catch him singing along to a song I never thought he would've liked otherwise. I cannot overstate how important these things are to a growing young man.

As a teenager, he eats and sleeps everything to do with sports, hunting, and fishing. He has a tight-knit friend group now, and they want to hunt and fish every chance they get. They make huge plans, with no money to pay for them and no transportation to get them there. As a father, I feel it is my duty to further instill this passion, so on many occasions, I will offer up my services as their driver and take them somewhere to fish. It is very special to see this fellowship bloom into true friendships through the outdoors. Sometimes, if we are at the hunting club to fish the little farm pond, I will just sit back and watch this unfold.

Seeing a bunch of teenagers, fishing as hard as they can, poking fun at one another and celebrating the victories of a fish caught, is a special sight. I can remember being this age, and how fascinating fishing trips could be. I love watching their friendships grow, knowing they have no idea that they are molding their futures much like I did at that age.

My father often played the same role that I do now. If I had a sleepover, we would always walk up the road to the old farm pond and try to catch a few bass. I recall at the time wondering if my dad was just taking us so he could go. Now, I realize what he was doing. He knew how important the outdoors had been in his life, and he wanted to make sure I had the same experiences. To this day, when I speak to an old friend, stories of fishing with my dad years ago often come up. He created core memories for us with such a seemingly small act.

• • •

I have always enjoyed the local cuisine of any area I visit. Part of the beauty of a hunt in Texas is the thought of a big ribeye cooked over fresh mesquite wood for dinner. The local Mexican ladies who cook for us on our trips to Laguna Madre always have something mind-blowing on the menu for every meal. The bush berries they pick and dice up to go on your steaks, or the secret green sauce they make using sour cream, olive oil, and fresh jalapeños seem to make every meal just a little more special.

One of my favorite experiences with local cuisine took place in Rhode Island. Three friends and I were in the state for a three-day duck hunt, along the coasts of Rhode Island and Massachusetts. Our guide was a great guy, and he loved the fellowship and food as much as anyone I had ever hunted with. One of the perks of his hunting operation was that he would offer a meal of all-you-can-eat lobster and steak one night at his house. He didn't offer lodging, so we were staying at a nearby hotel, but he offered his home to us on the last night of the hunt. That morning, after our hunt, he took us to a local seafood market to pick out some lobster.

At the time, we were four healthy-eating duck hunters who could eat all day. We were determined to put his "all you can eat" offer to the test. We picked out eight giant lobsters, one of which looked like it might have been exposed to some gamma radiation, as it had to have been 20 inches long, with claws the size of my fist.

When we showed up the night of the meal, we were greeted by his entire family and his assistant guide. They welcomed us into their home, fed us until we couldn't hold another morsel, then went to the freezer and pulled out a cheesecake. We stayed at their house til well past everyone's bedtime, getting to know one another. This was a truly special offer from someone who could have easily just taken our money for the hunts and made no attempt at true connection. I have never been a huge fan of lobster, but for some reason on this night, it was as fine as any five-star restaurant I have ever been to.

• • •

The beauty of a duck camp is often in its randomness. There will be a seventy-year-old retired professional, a twenty-year-old college student, two middle-aged guys getting away from their daily lives, and all else in between sitting around the same fire eating the same food. The lives lived by these guys couldn't be more different, but the common bond of what they're doing is all it takes. Some of the friends I have made in the last twenty years don't make sense on paper. But we love to chase ducks, and that's all it takes. One of my closest friends met an older, retired guy through a mutual friendship years ago. He loved to hunt, and loved to help build blinds and things of that sort, so we connected. Next thing I knew we were hunting together all the time. I keep up with his grandkids, and he asks about my kids. We text each other on birthdays, call just to check up, and look forward to our days together. A beautiful, random connection made through some fellowship at a duck club.

I have always viewed these chances at fellowship as benefits of my passion, but I now see them as opportunities I have been given. I am sharing myself, my passion, and often my family with total strangers, casual acquaintances, and lifelong friends. I have an opportunity to impact their lives with my input into their trip. My kindness, jokes, and the life perspective I offer have a chance to impact them long after they see me, and possibly long after I leave this world. What a gift, and how blessed I am. I have to make sure to take advantage of this, and try to make everyone's experience just a touch better by being there. This isn't my way of saying that my presence is a gift, but instead that my presence should be beneficial in some way. My goal should be to have the same impact on these people that they have on me. They are all special in my heart, so they deserve my very best when I am around.

CHAPTER 7

Life, Death, and Afterlife of an Outdoorsman

I am in an interesting chapter of my life, one where I'm experiencing my children in their younger years and my parents in their
older years. This provides a new perspective, as I am trying to give
my children opportunities to experience things for the first time
while also trying to provide my parents with opportunities to do
things for what could be the last time.

My dad gave me the idea to start an outdoors journal about
twenty years ago. Now, more than six hundred entries later, I am
so glad he put that bug in my ear. I can recall things in my head
pretty accurately, but when I look through the pages it is amazing
to see how many things I didn't even remember. A quick read of
a journal entry and it all floods back. Some of my favorite entries
now are the ones that include my father, myself, and my children.
Experiencing the outdoors with a grandparent is something I
never got to do. I've heard stories of my grandfathers' escapades,
and would love to have been able to witness them myself. My son
has been fortunate enough to sit in a deer stand with my father.
He has gotten to hunt deer and turkey with my wife's father, and
he always loves to fish with my wife's stepfather at his farm pond.
Now, in my sentimental life stage, this is more important than anything. I do my best to create these situations every chance I get,
and will continue to do that for as long as I can. I have two close
friends who have very healthy, active fathers in their seventies. I
get to hunt with one of them quite a bit, and I can see how much it
means to him being with his son as an adult. I wonder how many
opportunities to spend time together they would have missed in
their relationship if it weren't for duck hunting.

My hunting group of friends has a wide age range, and I see a lot of young kids these days, mostly children of my own friends. Seeing the smile on a kid's face as he sits behind his first turkey or deer is something special. The best part, which is often overlooked by most, is the pride seen in the fathers' faces at the same time. The attention is on the kids, but the dads are the ones truly making memories.

I feel like all of these kids are my family, and I have started to care more about their hunts these days. During this past duck season, one of my favorite little dudes got to shoot his first duck. Well . . . it was a drake hooded merganser, but nonetheless, he shot it himself. It was on a hunt I was asked to attend, but due to other obligations, I couldn't make it happen. As soon as I answered the phone that morning, he went straight into story mode. He is a very animated little man, and his stories are my favorite. I caught myself almost tearing up because I wasn't there to be a part of it with him.

That's how important these moments truly are. They are not just important because they are firsts; they are important because no one knows when it will be a last. Several years ago, back in the old swamp in Northampton that I've mentioned so many times, we had a pretty typical December duck hunt. My younger brother-in-law and a friend hunted one blind, while my older brother-in-law, another friend, and I hunted the other blind. The morning was fun, several mallards were shot, and lies were told.

The friend in my blind that morning was referred to by his friends as "Cheese." He was a truly special guy, always friendly to everyone and always happy. When I began spending time with my younger brother-in-law and his friends, I found a lot of new guys that I really enjoyed spending time with. At the top of this list, though, was Cheese. That man was always happy and excited about whatever the activity was. He loved a night at hunting camp, or a day out on the big water fishing for marlin. He was never scared of a good time, and naturally, we clicked. I always wanted him around because he had such a special aura about him, so I was excited to have him at the hunting camp that weekend. He couldn't care less about shooting that morning; he just wanted to be out there so he could talk some junk to his buddies. We had fun, but when we left, none of us could know how special that hunt would remain to us. With shock and deep sadness we realized it later that week, when Cheese passed unexpectedly. His last duck hunt was sitting beside me in what we refer to as the "big blind." We have a big picture framed of the guys from that hunt hanging at the cabin, and that memory is always there to remind us that we should make sure we enjoy all the hunts, because unfortunately, one of them is destined to be our last.

• • •

These first and lasts don't always refer to just the hunters involved, but also to their canine hunting companions. I was lucky enough to hunt with a good friend's pup one morning on what was essentially her first real hunt. We broke her in right, as she picked up a four-man limit, including pintails and black ducks and gadwall galore. She ended her morning with a 250-yard blind retrieve of a drake pintail, and all of us in the blind were cheering like she was winning the Daytona 500.

Having a dog hunt with you is another aspect of duck hunting that makes it all the more special. Hounds tracking deer and coons is special, watching them work chasing a coyote is something that would get any man excited, but those dogs are never truly with you on the hunt. A duck dog is sitting there, eyes to the sky the entire hunt. Every flock of birds, they're watching, every time you miss, they're judging, and every time it is slow, they are there for some snuggles and a snack.

I hunted with a good friend's dog for many years. That dog was a machine. Every time he left to go on a retrieve, no matter the circumstance, I knew he would return with the duck. He had a motor like no other and a nose that would match a bloodhound's. And best of all, once the day was over I could get him to come lie on the couch with me and fall sleep. It really did make the day that much better to watch the dog get to do what he loves, while we were all doing just that as well.

One summer, while the dog's owner was on vacation, the sitter found that the old dog had passed away in his garage. No signs of struggle; just a peaceful passing. Naturally, the owner, who happens to live next door to us, called me and his dad to bury him. We swapped some of the dog's old war stories and gave him a respectful burial. I can remember my last hunt with him on Lake Ellis at Camp Bryan, retrieving an afternoon wood duck. In fact, the pic of his final retrieve is the background photo on my laptop. It's another indicator of how special these relationships with our four-legged companions can be.

A very fine, touching proof of how strong the relationships among hunters and their dogs can be occurred a few years back. A tragic event took place while my son's yellow Lab was at training school, and he unexpectedly passed away at only twenty months old. Our family was crushed, especially my children. My son had been begging for a hunting dog, and we were in love with the big guy. Obviously, our extended family and friends in town had heard and expressed condolences, but we were going to move on and let this be a painful life lesson for all our family.

About three months later, a hunting buddy reached out and said he had to stop by my house. I welcomed him to stop by any-time. Now, mind you, this guy knows me only through outdoor activities, and that is the sole charter of our relationship. I hadn't seen or heard from him in a few months, so I was excited to see him.

When he stopped by, he handed me a framed painting, and all the emotions of the day we lost the Lab came flooding back. I immediately wept, and did everything I could to get myself together and hug my friend for such a gesture. You see, when my son's dog was alive, we took him along with us on a trip to Ocracoke for a week's vacation. I had posted a really awesome picture of my son, in shin-deep water on the sound side of the island. He was casting his fishing rod while his dog sat right beside him, watching his every move. This picture was already special to me, but I had no idea how special it could be. As it turns out, my hunting buddy's father is a painter. He painted this scene onto a canvas, and it looks so amazing. What a keepsake. That painting hangs by my front door to this day.

• • •

One of my journal entries is titled "Directions for When I Die." While that may sound morbid, there are things I want to be done to celebrate my life that the average person wouldn't even dream of. Not to get too detailed, but there are directions on how to handle my ashes; names of people I want to be able to send a message to, to make sure they feel my appreciation; and a note to my survivors directing them to pass my words along. That isn't intended to be some sort of note of things I am eager to see, but I have experienced enough in my life to know that I have no control over when my last day will be. I hope to see a duck blind in my eighties, take my great-grandchildren to a deer stand, and catch trout in a mountain stream much like I was able to do with my grandmother a few years ago. Unfortunately, hopes and dreams like these don't typically come to see the light of day. On the chance that they do not, sharing my experiences is what I can hope to accomplish in the rest of my years.

I do not believe myself to be a man of much legacy. I won't be remembered as some CEO of a company, or for saving the world with my philanthropy. I am simply a simple man. I have tried to live my life with some purpose, and the older I get, the more I see God's work all around me and inside me. My legacy will come from the little things I did. My kids will be able to read my journals; my contributions to Ducks Unlimited will have made some difference; the kids I have coached will, I hope, remember the fun they had; and my friends will remember a guy who loved to hunt and loved his friends and family. My legacy will be those people, my family and friends. I hope to know that someday, in some random duck blind, way after I am gone, my name will come up in some story about a hunt I was a part of, or some young kid will remember me cheering them on when they made their first water swat. I hope my kids will remember me as a dad who tried really hard, through tons of failure and effort. I see my flaws every day, and I try to fix them, but I am simply that—flawed. I want to spend the rest of my days doing what I love with the people I love, and that's it. Hopefully that web of friends will continue to grow, and I can continue to see new places. God knows I can't wait to do just that!

• • •

As the years have come and gone, I have slowly started to revert back to my roots more than ever before. I grew up in the church, attending every Wednesday and Sunday with my family. As I got older, I grew away from the church and started leading a path that wasn't always full of the best decisions and life choices. As I started a family, a passion inside me led me back to the church. Initially, I wanted to ensure that my children were provided the same experiences that I had. I knew that the lessons of Jesus's stories were important, but still, I was simply going through the motions.

Over the past several years, my view of religion has changed dramatically. The stories of the Bible ring more true in my ears now than ever before. I want to learn more and live my life in a way that a true Christian would.

The term "Christian" has been used a lot lately for political reasons, and lots of average Americans now have a mistaken view of what a Christian is supposed to be. A man who uses the term "Christianity" to justify an action, or to make himself seem to be a more honorable person, is not what I think of when I hear the term. A Christian is supposed to live his life in a way that depicts Christ-like behavior. You can go to church three days a week, and still not fit this description.

I have recently found myself in a men's Bible study, led by two of the best, truest Christians I have ever met. We meet in a banquet room, where we eat and discuss things that affect men and how to deal with them the proper way. This has filled a void I had recently noticed in my heart. I have learned so much about the fellowship of Christ, and I want to do my part to spread that to the other groups of men I am lucky enough to spend time with.

Growing up, I saw the men of my life actively playing a role in my church life. As I grew to be a man, I developed a skewed view of these men. My dad played drums in the church band and my uncle was a deacon. Often, I saw them as flawed men, even though I loved them dearly. I often thought, if these guys can be representatives of Jesus, then I guess anybody can. I almost saw it as a slight to the church.

Suddenly, though, one of the most recent mule kicks of my

life hit right in the chest. This is why the church is so important. Anyone can be impactful, anyone can make a difference, and anyone can walk that path. I am not a perfect man by any means. I enjoy a bourbon on Saturday evening after a good hunt, I often get frustrated with my children and probably overreact and speak in an unforgiving tone, I even tend to cuss like a sailor from time to time when I get excited.

I am aware of these things, along with others, but the Lord's work can still be done through my flawed body. Speaking with the men of my Bible study, I see that the men I have often viewed as "perfect" are just as flawed as I am. The difference is that they go out of their way to make a difference. They offer themselves in service to others, and act in a way that can be respected by anyone they are around. Simply being there for someone is all it takes sometimes, but having the bravery to also share your feelings in return is special. Seeing this group of men from all walks of life opening up about their feelings and supporting one another is something I am proud to be a part of.

. . .

I hold countless memories of times sitting in the woods with my dad and my uncle, looking at nothing in particular, just soaking in the nature all around us. In those moments, both of those flawed, Godly men would say "This is what it's all about. This is as good as church to me; this is where I feel God the most." As a young man, you often just nod your head in agreement, as my son does to me now.

The words lodged in there somehow, though. The older I get, the more those memories and those lessons tend to creep out of the corners of my mind. These mule kicks I have referred to throughout this book are the Lord's way of connecting some wires in my head to remind me of what life is about.

I have been blessed with a huge network of friends that I can influence. Through my actions and my words, the Lord's presence in me is something I hope they can at least appreciate. Furthermore, there is still room for me to do more. I want these friends to think of me in the same light in which I think of my Bible study leaders, and the only way to do that is to continue to improve and act in a way that leads to the positive light. I can share these amazing places throughout God's playground with these same people, and many, many more.

What an opportunity I have right at my fingertips. Experiences in nature can truly show you the wonder of God's world. Sitting in a deer stand with my son last year, as the sun set and we watched more than thirty whitetails going about their natural lives in every direction, I whispered to him, "This is what it's all about, this is where you can truly see God's work." He nodded, much like I probably did thirty years ago, but he heard it.

• • •

The therapy of putting these words on paper has brought me to a point of no longer wanting to maintain my life as it is. I can see through these pages that I have been so blessed, and I have so much to offer. I don't mean that I am going to go out as an evangelist and change the world. That isn't my style. But what I can do is continue to realize the effect I am capable of having, and make sure I take advantage of every opportunity I am presented with. I need to be out there, with my friends, and their family and friends, and continue to grow my connections. I want people to remember me for all the flaws I carry and all the good I can offer. If I can pull that off, maybe I can do enough to pay back all of these amazing prizes the Lord has already awarded to me. I am not yet a man who feels comfortable sharing my experiences with God and the Word of God directly. This is something that takes some practice, and as far as I am concerned, I am just learning the rules.

What I do know, though, is what I am sharing with others in our time outdoors is so special and so overwhelming, I need to at least make that point known. Being in God's creation, seeing a sunrise on a cold winter's morning, or watching a sunset right after an afternoon thunderstorm on a river in August is not something to be seen as common. Even if you see it every day, it is just as awe-inspiring the four hundredth time as it was the on the first. Seeing a flock of teal lock up in your decoys at first light, or a turkey strut into your food plot midmorning, is something that comes directly from the hand of God as a gift.

Yes, we may have planted the food plot, or built the duck blind, or even got some intel from a trail camera, but we were still given a moment so awesome that it needs to be shouted from the rooftops. Sharing your hunting stories is akin to sharing God's word, if done the right way.

• • •

Compassion and appreciation are something an outdoors-man must practice. It is hard for a non-hunter to understand all the work that goes into conservation and land management. They often see it as a means for slaughter, but that is not the case. When an ethical hunter kills an animal, it is a sacred moment. That animal lived a beautiful life, and he or she had no idea how much they mattered to us. We, as hunters, spend countless hours thinking about them, studying pictures of them on trail cameras, talking about them, and using all of our skills to put ourselves in a position to harvest them. It is hard not to feel true compassion when you see an animal that you killed. You do your best to show respect, and make sure that you enjoy the animal's meat and use the act of hunting as a chance to grow closer with nature.

Seeing baby wood ducks come from a box I put up in a swamp doesn't make me eager to shoot them in the fall; it only makes me appreciate their presence even more. It is the same with any other animals that benefit from this conservation; I want to see all of God's creatures thrive. This thought process seems confusing to those who do not hunt. It can easily be viewed as an alpha male activity, where the death of the animal is the only reward. A true outdoorsman wants to leave the woods better than they found it. We listen to podcasts about new studies on populations, we plant year-round food sources, and we even donate our hard-earned money through the purchases of licenses to the cause.

If it weren't for the painstaking work and conservation efforts of the American outdoorsman, hundreds of species would no longer be with us. A true man of the land wants not only to harvest an animal, but to have so many of them thriving in his area that his harvest is actually a means of management. It is quite an accomplishment to find ourselves in that situation. Killing a wild animal is a serious event. We love these creatures. Old deer are around on camera so long they get names. Mature ducks are so gorgeous in your hand that it's often a topic of discussion while you hold your fresh kill. A turkey can be so smart and cunning for so long that the thought of him being gone after a successful hunt can almost be grief-inducing.

Sharing the stories of a hunt in the glory of what the event truly is—that is how the beauty of the animals' lives is preserved. You must appreciate every moment like this. As a hunter who spends what some may consider to be too many days in the field, it can become easy to take these moments and these animals for granted. That's when you have to step back and soak it in. God's love is not only in your heart, but all around you in the things he allows you to experience.

CHAPTER 8

Another Season Closes

As I write these pages, I am in the midst of reflecting on what was recently the last weekend of duck season. The Lord sent me one last, extra-hard mule kick, and I am certain it was no coincidence. My previous chapters were finished, and I thought I stood behind a complete work, or at least the best I could offer. Then, thanks to my understanding wife and great friends, I experienced a

thirty-hour trip that included examples of everything I have discussed in this writing.

One of my closest friends and his dad invited me and two other
great friends down to Camp Bryan for the final day of the season. I
hadn't been down to camp in a while, so I was excited enough with
that. Then, my friends made it so much more exciting. The friend
who invited me has been one of my closest hunting buddies for
more than ten years. Probably 50 percent of the ducks I have ever
shot came while sitting right beside him. His dad is also one of my
favorites to hunt with. He's getting older, but his motor is always
ready. He loves to shoot and watch a dog work. One of the other
friends is someone I see and hunt with a lot, as he lives in town,
but we rarely duck hunt together. The last guy is a great friend, and
we talk nearly every day, but he lives across the state and we hadn't
duck hunted together in nearly three years. Ducks or no ducks, I
knew this was going to be a special day in the blind.

The night before the hunt, the camp hosted a huge oyster
roast. More than forty folks were there, gathered to celebrate the
last day of the club's season. I saw folks I hadn't seen in years, and
some I see somewhat often. I met new people who shared common friends, and we told stories and laughed and ate. Later, a few
of us went back to our friend's house, got a fire going, and started
cooking some meat and listening to music. We had the four of us
middle-aged guys, three guys in their twenties, and two dads over
sixty all sitting around the fire, in true fellowship. We told stories
of the season, of past seasons, and shared our hopes for future
seasons. My Amazon music would randomly play a song that got

everyone's attention, and we would sing together. Because I had been secretly writing this book over the previous several months, all of these instances really stood out to me. The emotions from these pages were still flowing through my head like the clear, tumbling water of an NC mountain stream.

The next morning, we headed to a fairly new location, a deep-water impoundment I had never gotten the opportunity to hunt before. It was unseasonably warm, 65 degrees with a south wind, so we knew the conditions were less than ideal. Nonetheless, the birds flew all morning. We made some great shots, and saw some great dog work. The friend whose dog I buried had been hunting his new Lab for the past two seasons. That dog is really starting to come into his own. Seeing them bond, and the dog succeed in some tough situations, was awesome. We shot plenty, but we finished with six ducks left to our limit, as we didn't want to see it end so quickly.

We went in for a quick lunch, then decided to watch the duck season end at his new impoundment about an hour away. We all left separately, so I wasn't following anyone. I wasn't sure of the best route, so I threw the address in my Google Maps and took off. About twenty minutes in, I realized that I was about to get on a ferry. I was the only one who made this error, but instead of turning around and backtracking, I just went with it.

And how happy I was that I did. That ferry ride turned out to be a special part of that day, and I would never have gotten to experience it without a little bit of accidental magic. There were bluebills all over the river, the sun was warm, and the water was beautiful. I was only about fifteen minutes late when I arrived at the impoundment, and we all headed to a blind. It was comfortable, and we were all in T-shirts, still a bit warm.

As we walked in, we jumped about forty to fifty ducks out of the impoundment. As they exited over the back corner, we watched as a hawk came out of one of the pines in a surprise attack and took a wood duck right out of the sky—something I have never seen before and will likely never see again.

The action that afternoon was steady, as wood ducks and the occasional mallard gave us some attention. We finished our limits, and it did not go unappreciated. I rolled out a beautiful drake wood duck as my last shot of the season. I saw the dog make a great blind retrieve on a bird that fell in some thick stuff. He came out with that duck in his mouth practically smiling, covered from head to toe in cockleburs, and we all cheered him on as he returned.

As the sun set, we knew it was over. As my buddy and I picked up the decoys for the last time, we didn't really speak. I wasn't sad, just reflecting. Every year I say, "This was the best season yet," knowing good and well the best season is always the next one.

This time though, I really soaked it in. That crossing wood duck with my buddy's 28-gauge could be the last duck I ever shoot, and it could be the last time I share a blind with one of my friends. Although it sounds morbid, it wasn't that at all. For once, I took in the moment for how precious and special it was. We watched the swans fly over from the bank and shared stories of the evening until it got too dark to see.

My friend had also invited two other friends, one of them his old dog trainer and the other a buddy a bit older than we were who had recently started duck hunting. At the ripe age of fifty-six, he'd shot his first-ever wood duck that afternoon. You couldn't wipe the smile off his face, or anyone else's for that matter.

This is what it is all about—experiences shared with like-minded people from all walks of life. As I got into the truck to head home, the first song that came on my radio was "Soulshine." I thought of a great buddy I haven't hunted with in a few years and wished he had been with us. As a perfect ending to a great trip, God had sent me one last reminder to not let time get in the way of all of these friendships. I look forward to calling that friend and catching up. This is just the beginning of my journey.

ACKNOWLEDGMENTS

First off, I want to thank my wife, Katie, for always pushing me to put my words out there in some way. She never thought I was crazy for wanting to write a book. She only saw my vision and wanted to see it come true.

Also, thank you to my kids for providing me with so many opportunities for stories and reflection. Their presence at these events is what triggered the sentimental section of my brain to really start enjoying the moments for what they are.

Without my parents and family, I would have never been able to live out this life, which has become so full of experiences. My mom and dad pushed me to do what I love, and were with me all along the way. My Uncle Doug has always been there, making every event a little more fun than it would have been otherwise. My in-laws are also just as important as anyone. My father-in-law took me under his wing from day one and has allowed both me and my family to enjoy some amazing opportunities.

Friends and fellow GU members, you know who you are. I am sure you read some stories in here that sounded familiar, and I thank you for making memories with me.

Finally, thank you to Bill Fentress. When I got started on this journey, I realized that Bill and I had some mutual friends, and

I had enjoyed his book *The Yellow Honeysuckle is the Sweetest* so much. When I reached out, I was greeted with a warm welcome and answers to all my questions. Not only that, but he also encouraged me to finish the project, because he knew it could be something special.